SACRIFICED LIFE

English Translation of
Partha Mere Hisse Ka Aakash

MOHAN LAL MISHRA 'DHEERAJ'

TRUE SIGN
PUBLISHING HOUSE

Published by True Sign Publishing House
Address: SY. No. 21/2 & 21/3, Sonnenahalli,
Krishnarajapura, Bengaluru,
Karnataka - 560049 India
E-mail: truesignbooks@gmail.com
Website: www.truesign.in

Sacrificed Life
English Translation of
Partha Mere Hisse Ka Aakash
Author: Mohan lal Mishra 'Dheeraj'

ISBN: 978-93-5584-141-4

First Edition: 2022

Two Words

Shri Mohan lal Mishra 'Dheeraj' is a famous Hindi Actor, dramatist, and storyteller. Inspired by Indian culture, universalism, and national consciousness, his works have been written keeping idealism in the centre. I am fortunate to have the distinction of being the first reader of each of his works. The anomalies and squalors prevailing in the society,

He has known criminal characters while in government service and later in the form of legalism and he has been successful in conveying the message to the society by revealing them through his fiction. The specialty of 'Dheeraj' ji is that he finds the formula of life even in all those opposing tendencies. This ideal and optimism may seem somewhat hostile in today's era, but this optimism of Dheeraj ji is the lifeblood of literature.

This sequence of 'Dheeraj' ji is also present in his novel 'Parth Mere Hisse Ka Akash' to be published. This novel is also present in the present era verbal problem terrorism. This novel is the result of the deep concern of the creator towards the global problem of the present era, terrorism. This concern of the creator devoted to his era and society is natural. In this novel, the narrator has researched its manifestation and nurture more than the consequences of terror. Without identifying the seed, we cannot stop its growth. Through this novel, the author has investigated all those social and constitutional institutions, whose work is the structure of a healthy society. The characters in this novel are modern

But their names are associated with mythological references. From the Mahabharata to the horrors of two world wars, how can violence be stopped in this world and how the welfare of the living being should be, this is the concern of the author. Written in amazing theatrical style. The story is collectible and readable.

My heartiest congratulations to Dheeraj ji for this latest novel.

Dated - 01.11.2020

Dr. Laxmi Kant 'Pandey'
Chief Editor
NAVNIKASH
Monthly Magagine
Kanpur
9452694078

Wishing For World Welfare

Mohan lal Mishra 'Dheeraj' Ji's novel was written keeping the problem of terrorism prevalent in many countries of the world in the centre. For the last almost 30 years, our country has been suffering from this problem. Dheeraj Ji has given a vivid depiction of human tendencies with reference to the characters of Mahabharata. There is a flow in the plot which keeps the reader hooked. Partha, the character of the novel, is a symbol of an amazing life, just as trees do not grow on the mountains, but a very small tree grows. Life expectancy is the mother of willpower. The basic purpose of the plot is the wish of the author for all welfare, world peace, and world welfare. The novel is very interesting, educative, and public welfare from every point of view. Certainly, the novel will be welcomed in the literary field. It is my belief.

Dated - 10.10.2020

Dr. Satish Chandra Sharma 'Sudhanshu'
Editor-in-Chief "New Horizons"
Patrika, Brahmapuri, Bisauli,
Badaun

In My Point View

The great playwright of Hindi literature, story novelist Mr. Mohan Lal Mishra by 'Dheeraj', Parth Mere Part Ka Akash is presented in front of the public, through this novel, the way the author has deeply hurt the mentality of the common Indian citizen, it is really reprehensible. This reflects how the author has depicted the violent form of molten fire as an image. This novel will leave a unique impression in the heart of the readers, where it will tickle it inside, while it will also try to erase the misconception in the mind. I do not only hope but have full faith that this novel of Mohan ji will be respected in the literary world.

Dated - 10.10.2020

Dr. Vijay Kumar Pandey
F/128 Panki Kanpur

Good Wishes

Agraj Shriyut Mohan Lal Mishra 'Dheeraj', rich in multidimensional talent, has written many books on various burning problems. He has written and staged many plays. He is also a successful theatre artist. After being actively associated with the legal profession, he has done literary service, which is worthy of praise.

Dheeraj's new novel Parth Mere Hisse Ka Akash is a novel of its kind. Presently the whole world is battling terrorism. Most of the country is worried. UNO is also giving guidelines on this. But after that terrorism could be controlled by only a few percent. Terrorist incidents are happening every day. Keeping this subject matter in mind, Parth Mere Hisse Ka Akash ' has been written.

The protagonist of the novel, Captain Parth, reveals many hidden mysteries. Corruption is also rampant in the Defence Ministry, in which big officials and leaders are involved, due to which the country is in the transition of crisis, due to which the country has come in the transition period crisis. In a way, it falls under the category of the detective novel.

Waiting for more new work from Dheeraj Ji's writing.

With best regards, I wish you a healthy and long life.

Dated - 04.09.2020

Advocate Ajendra Awasthi
President Rotary Club Unnao
M. No. 9415076060

New Vision

The name of Shri Mohan lal Mishra 'Dheeraj' is taken with great respect in the advocate cadre, government employees' organizations, and literary world. While busy with legal business and doing organizational work, he continues to practice literature continuously. He has a simple and generous-hearted personality. I have shared this with Dheeraj ji in many forums. He is a poet, writer, and playwright as well as a brilliant orator. He has gifted me many books for Mahatma Gandhi Library Unnao - Bhavna, Chauraha, Radha Mahlav, Pravasi Maitri, Sparsh, and one more Rama, etc.

Parth Mere Hisse Ka Akash's novel will prove to be a milestone in the literary world in the coming tomorrow if the reader will be compelled to read the novel once. The curiosity of the reader remains from beginning to end.

In the novel, the special places of the famous foreign city from Unnao, Kanpur Banda have been described in a quick manner.

In this novel, there are visions of his long-term literary practice. You will also get a glimpse of Indian culture. also accepted the principle of ancestral birth

The protagonist of this novel is Captain Parth. Through his character, society has tried to give a message to the country and the world, which is completely welcome.

Only a writer is capable of changing the direction and condition of society, country, and the world. Expresses respect.

Dated - 04.09.2020

Kaushalendra Mishra 'Atul'
Date 28 September 2020
General Secretary, Sahitya Bharti
Mahatma Gandhi Library
UNNAO

To A New Dimension

The present novel "Parth Mere Hisse Ka Akash" does not support terrorism, but expresses deep concern over its birth and nurture. The answer contained in the question is whether the government treats the ruling public with unconstitutionally cruel treatment with ruthless killings for its own personal interest. In such a situation, it is necessary to take timely, well-intentioned decisions with understanding in doing justice to the constitutional institutions, the serious question is, are the institutions so powerful in ensuring the compliance of the given decision?

Exploration of Universal Truth Different religious communities and institutions of the world contemplate in the periphery of their own beliefs, traditions, beliefs, ideas, and beliefs, but although all the objectives are the same, there is no consensus. Indian literary literature, which is filled with the concept of Sarvahitaya, is following the policy of religious equality, but some such religious sects and institutions consider it their sacred duty to commit genocide in an attempt to prove themselves the best. This is the main subject of contemplation, which is standing in front of the whole world as a question? This situation has been going on for a long time, that is why we must take a bird's eye view of various religious texts.

The events happening at present on the world stage are creating a crisis for human life. Some problems are man created/ made, some are natural born. We have to study both and work together in a planned manner to solve them.

Once studied in Sociology—

"Criminals are not born but made"

It is relevant today.

The environment affects the individual, family, society, country, and the whole world, that is, ideological thinking which presents new dimensions.

All the characters in this novel are fictional. If the name and event have a resemblance with someone, then it will be called a coincidence.

The study of religious sects, schools, traditions prevalent in different regions, countries, and many plots became very necessary in the present environment.

The First World War, the Second World War, and many wars took place, resulting in destruction, massacres, and the gruesome voice of hatred and hatred came to the fore. In the midst of these, a reflection on the action plan of the soldiers devoted to the nation and the role of the government, opposition, and public will be found in it.

Through the characters of the novel, the different human tendencies have been engraved with words for the welfare of the world.

There should be no third world war, world peace should be established, this is the invocation of this novel.

I express my gratitude to those who have contributed directly or indirectly in writing my novel.

Adversity blocks the way; Struggle makes the way; Resolve not to give up in life is the invocation of life. The thinking of the human group also changes nature. There is compatibility in positive thinking. But with negative thinking, nature becomes unfavourable and creates divine disaster. This is a universal principle.

I express my best wishes to my readers. Respect and gratitude to all the savvy readers who established the author.

Love, justice, and truth are synonymous with God. The novel "Parth-Mere Hisse Ka Akash" presented for world welfare is presented.

Do send your feedback after reading.

I salute all the great souls who have sacrificed their lives for the sake of the world. Dedicated to the vision of world welfare.

Dated - 06.02.2020

Yours
Mohan Lal Mishra 'Dheeraj'
9451110945

Review

I had read the story collection "Vicharo Ke Badal" by the author of the novel "Parth Mere Hisse Ka Akash", Mohan Lal Mishra, "Dheeraj", then after reading the stories I realized that the writer is very upset with the discrepancies in the society. Very distressed by the pain of selfishness, the humiliation of the elderly, character degradation, etc. because he has shown the same pain in his writing. The author reaches the heart of the readers. The author of the novel "Parth Mere Hisse Ka Akash" presented by Mr. Mohan Lal Mishra is endowed with multidimensional talent.

Novelist, story writer, proficient in many genres! The novelist has successfully tried to convey the message of public welfare to the readers through the characters of the novel. The author's pen says a lot about socialism, familyism, communism, dynastic Marxism, etc., which gives an idea and thought. The novel does not support terrorism but what does the experience of terrorist suffering? How dangerous is it for society?, How are everyone's feelings hurt? He has made this point very easily!

Extremism terrorism thrives under the shelter of the government, how terrorists attack the country, the right warrior does not get his respect, only polymaths take away the respect.

In a very simple language, how they have created a beautiful bouquet by weaving pearls of words into the fabric of problems like exploitation, abduction, etc. of women in the society!

The author has marked every episode related to terror very easily. The author has a keen eye and a penchant for the activities of Babas.

He has raised every anomaly of the society and left one question before the public to think,

His writings have also presented the culture and religious communities of different provinces in great detail. The writer's pen is filled with the spirit of upliftment of the society and welfare of the people. Positive thoughts only make a person (writer) great. The author has adopted a very liberal style in some places.

Regarding the burning problems of today's times, the hero of the novel, Parth, has been portrayed very beautifully. The author worked very hard and studied, he has done justice to the world war, epidemic and has expressed his pain, the novel moves with beautiful word combination and flow in simple language, successful in keeping the reader hooked. There will be a constant curiosity as to what will happen next........?

I wish the author the very best, you continue to write like this and keep giving rich and high-quality literature to Hindi literature, I wish you good health with endless best wishes and keep your pen going like this.

Dr. Alka Pandey
Mumbai National President
All India Agni Shikha Forum
9920899214

Partha Mere Hisse ka Akash

The presented novel does not support terrorism, but while expressing serious thought, says that the small and big nations of the world should write a new light.

Dedicated
to the invisible power,
the lord of all the constants
of the entire universe

Cruel governments in the name of governance, crossing the limits of injustice, cruel behaviour on the public:

Secret treaties and funding by certain states with terrorist organizations: Suspicious role or weakness of the United Nations and the use of veto power.

The treaties made for the interests of the nations, the chapter of history, in the above context, serious reflection on the future policy for the welfare of the world.

Terrorist organization

Such inhuman organizations commit ruthless killings of innocent people, misinterpreting religion and committing murders in the name of jihad. In these contexts, the possibilities of third world war and epidemic are being reflected. Dedicated to all the nations and organizations who embody the feelings of "Vasudhaiv- Kutumbaka" for the benefit of the world, the novel- Partha Mere Hisse Ka Akash.

Mystery

What is there is not visible and what is seen is actually not. Vanshika dialed a number from her mobile.

A new musical sound was heard on the mobile number dialed - Shri Ram Jai Ram, Jai -Jai Ram.

Along came a voice, the person you are calling is busy on another call. Please call after a while, thank you.

On dialing the number again, the same reply was received. Her restlessness was increasing. He had to give important information. Meanwhile, the servant brought tea and biscuits to the table and said, "madam, please drink your tea." She gestured to go out by placing tea in his ear with his hand attached to the mobile.

It was seven in the morning. She was sitting in her furnished room after doing exercise, bathing, and meditation. The room was rectangular. The length was much greater than the width. There was a cupboard on one side, in which books of some great writers were kept along with the books of law. The cupboards had transparent glasses. The books were decorated in such a way that the name of that book and the name of its author could be read easily. In the other corner, two feet away from the door, a man-sized mirror was hanging on the wall. On a large table, on which was placed the glass with the top down, on which it could be written. A small size rack on the left side of the table on which some important books are kept. There was a pen stand in the middle, in which many colored ink pens, dot-pens were kept. Vanshika was sitting on the chair who wanted to talk to the mobile but could not talk.

When someone wants to convey very important information to a particular person but gets restless in case of non-communication, there are many reasons for that. Problems of communication devices, adverse weather conditions. Sometimes sending secret information has to be spelled with great care, otherwise, there is every possibility of the entire warp of the target being shattered.

The form of 'Vanshika' is very attractive. Height 5 feet 8 inches which is more than normal female. The beauty of the body flourished habitually through yoga and exercise. Big eyes, almond complexion, beautiful nose, lips like two petals of a rose mixed together. Teeth Like a pomegranate seed, a sharp tooth on the right side is nice to see when she laughs. Whether she speaks Hindi or English, whenever she speaks, she says something in a rhythm, the meaning of saying is fluent. It is clear from his speech that along with being a great speaker, the qualities of a great commander are also reflected.

She finally opened up her computer - a study report from a US university released by the US State Department on June 02, 2016. According to the report prepared by Maryland University, there has been some decrease in the number of terrorist incidents and deaths in the world since 2015 as compared to the year 2014.

She started studying further on the computer to know the main points of the story.

The five countries most affected by terrorism include India, Pakistan, Iraq, Afghanistan and Nigeria - American University Report.

Terrorist incidents in the world in 2015 compared to prior (2014), according to this report prepared by the University of Maryland, released by the State Department on June 02, 2016, in a university study report on the status of terrorism in various countries. There has been some reduction in the death toll from them. The following are the main notable points of this report:

In the year 2015, 92 people of the world are victims of some kind of terrorist incident.

- There has been a 13 percent reduction in terrorist incidents recorded in 2015 as compared to the previous year 2014.
- The trend of reduction in the number of terrorist incidents and deaths has been going on since 2012, in contrast, there has been an increase in the number of terrorist attacks and deaths in 2015 in Afghanistan, Bangladesh, Egypt, Syria, and Turkey.
- During 2015, 74% of total deaths due to terrorist incidents occurred in five countries Iraq, Afghanistan, Nigeria, Syria.

In this report of the University of Maryland, it has been told that at present, the terrorist organization IS has emerged as the biggest challenge in the world and it has occupied a large area in Iraq and Syria.

Vanshika set off her laptop and started thinking, how to warn the French government that the incident should stop......

In the code, circuit cell 03 was informed that dark clouds can rain at any time.

The Secret Cell (Intelligence Department) keeps on alerting the country from time to time about important institutions.

Today the whole world is trapped in a web of illusions. Small and big nations have their own problems and agendas.

Dynasticism, Familism, Socialism, Marxism, Communism, and Theism, etc. have their own streams, and due to the contradiction in these contexts in their schools – there is a situation of conflict. Ram Rajya is accepted as the best system. Here is his religion with dynasty. Respecting the sentiments of the people, the governance system should be run, this is Ram Raj.

Vanshika's restlessness was increasing. The security officers have to work by respecting the intention of the government, keeping in mind the orders of the United Nations of the country, but terrorist organizations have nothing to do with it. Sometimes in special circumstances, they also do what terrorists would do for the national interest.

Here this point is worth considering, what is the credibility of the government in these situations? How did Captain Partha get caught in the clutches of the conspirators on the web? On the one hand, the government was directing for his court-martial. On the other hand, terrorist organizations had become enemies of his life. That Partha was asking for his share of the sky, there was a very complicated restlessness.

Events that happen, will continue to happen. From the beginning till today, the game of life and death has been going on and will continue. Nothing is new but there is repetition, but new continues to happen.

Whatever it is today is the result of karma through the processes done in the past.

Every living being in the world, land, water, and air and material-conscious are all governed by the invisible supreme power, due to the division of this supreme power, good and bad events happen. Somewhere people do collective worship, meditation, some people are seen engaged in service for the benefit of mankind. Some people commit mass atrocities. Both have different results. In this sequence, the link of a story is added.

There are many religious discourses in the world, all aimed at human welfare.

The question is that there were many wars in the name of religion. The question is what exactly is religion?

Events happen, but there must be a reason behind it.

Is the purpose of man peace or war? This question is so disturbing, so disturbing that the mind of the best-learned warrior is unable to decide whether to fight or make a treaty or leave everything and go elsewhere.

In Dwapar, Sadhvi Kunti questioned the incarnation of Yog-yogeshwar Lord Krishna, the incarnation of sixteen arts-

Again, people consider you as the form of God and Vishnu avatar, can't you stop this Mahabharata war?

Shri Krishna said, "I can certainly stop the war, but I will not."

"Why after all?"

"Honorable Bua ji, like the laws of this world, there are rules, in this way there are universal laws and regulations of nature. The result of the actions performed by the living beings is automatically certain to happen. The reward of the actions without any discrimination It is my compulsion to plan. I cannot interfere in the works of nature. War is definitely possible." Sometimes war becomes necessary.

Lord Shri Krishna said- "Bua, you can ask me for a boon"

The holy Kunti said- "If you give me a problem, then also give me the wisdom to solve the problem."

Lord Shri Krishna said - "Avamstu, the cycle of Kalachakra continues on its own without stopping continuously. Events keep happening moment by moment."

For some reason, the thought of solitude and retirement and the thought of suicide came in the mind of Colonel Bhishma Narayan Sharma, Captain Partha, Vinay, when at the same time he should have faced the circumstances by living in the world. Such situations sometimes come in the life of every living being.

Adversity blocks the way, struggle makes the way. The Time cycle has its own speed.

He was plunged into the darkness of utter despair. He could not be contacted by anyone. All the means of communication were denied to him. Such situations come into the lives of many people. That state of mind also has to be considered. When a person, despite being innocent, is implicated in a planned manner by conspiracy, while he is free from guilt. There are many reasons to implicate someone. For example, when the individual/

organization/country considers others to be fatal for themselves for criminal tendency and self-fulfillment, the threat of their own existence arises while they are alive.

Captain Partha was an honest, hard-working, intelligent, and tactful military officer. He was surrounded like Abhimanyu of Mahabharata. Behind him was death. He was not able to decide how to get out of this Chakravyuha?

Resistance - Struggle

Partha
my part of the sky
action-reaction action
life death
live life
and death again life

Guru Dronacharya, a great scholar, the best archer, made all the Kauravas and Pandavas proficient in the education of war skills with his intellect. In Guru Dakshina, he asked King Drupada to be taken prisoner and presented before him.

He knew very well that only Partha, my supreme disciple, could do this work for my benefit.

Vinayak: - He is narrating the context of the Adi Parva of Mahabharata to Vandana. Vandana is pregnant.

On the instructions of Bhishmanarayan Sharma, it was reciting the story of Lakshman Ram, Krishna, and Arjuna and the great heroes and their character with veneration.

Furnished room all the beauty displayed items were kept in place by planning. A very beautiful picture of Radhakrishna is kept in the cupboard. Lord Krishna is playing flute in tribhangi posture. Nearby Param Sundari Radherani's picture with calm charming eyes, Kamdhenu, cow dancing and peacock's back ground in light blue color on the back.

Vinayak sitting on a comfortable chair, Vandana is lying on a double bed with the help of a village pillow. The month of November is neither too hot nor too cold. fine weather. Mercury tube has milky light. Ceiling fan is running on number two. The calm form of Vandana is like Maa Kaushalya.

Her skin was white and soft like curd, pale pink color was scattered on his cheeks. There was a sweet smile on the delicate lips like two petals of a rose, a landscape of pleasure-less, lust-filled, blissful feeling of ultimate bliss. At this time Vandana was wearing a Coca-Cola-coloured sari. Her

SACRIFICED LIFE

beauty was increasing with a blouse of the same color. Her face was seen glowing with an aura of silent love. That form is reflected in the meditation of yogis as Mahalakshmi. The color of the bed sheet on which she was lying was sea light blue and the shape of flowers and leaves were visible on it. Vinayak while caressing Vandana's cheek said, "Blessed, very beautiful future, tomorrow's future is nurtured in your holy womb." Vandana did not oppose Vinayak's touch, but spoke silently with her charming eyes - "What is this? Take the statement forward."

Vinayak never did any discourse before this, nor story reading, story reading, discourse is an art. The speaker narrates the story compiled in his mood in an interesting way - the audience sitting in front listens to the mantra with awe. The simple story, according to the time, along with the musical tale, kirtan, keep changing, according to that, does the whole universe change in the human race.

Vinayak never did any discourse before this, nor story reading, story reading, discourse is an art. The speaker narrates the story compiled in his mood in an interesting way - the audience sitting in front listens to the mantra with awe. The simple story, according to the time, along with the musical tale, kirtan, keep changing, according to that, does the whole universe change in the human race.

Today the clouds of the whole world war have started hovering in most of the countries, the internal system is disturbed, civil war is going on. Big countries do not want to compete among themselves, but to establish supremacy in the world generated by the spirit of the country.

At this time, an identity of India has been made on the world stage. There are many reasons for that. The root cause is Indian literary literature. First of all, the story of the origin of Vedas was from divine power, but study of Vedas and Shudras were prohibited. No comments on this. It is noteworthy that the first poet Trikalgya Maharishi Valmiki described the glory of the character of Rama in the holy book Ramayana. Who is able to guide the whole world.

In this series - Mahabharata, the epic is a priceless treasure of literary literature in Sanskrit. It is named in the scriptures as the fifth Veda. This is not only the true and comprehensive history of India, as it is expressed in its name, as well as it has a very poignant and succinct discussion of all subjects like religion, knowledge, dispassion, devotee yoga, ethics, spirituality, politics etc. It will not be an exaggeration if it is called the encyclopedia of Indian knowledge. Its author, Maharishi Krishna Dwaipayana Ved Vyas ji has said about it with his mouth.

"Yennehasti na mischarchit"-

The topic which has not been discussed in it is not available anywhere else.

Priceless like Shrimad Bhagwat Geeta

A gem with an invaluable name like Shrimad Bhagwat Geeta is also a gift of this ocean. Many great poets of change have composed their immortal epics and plays by making it fertile. In total there are one lakh verses in it. That is why it is called 'Shat Sahasri Samhita'. Initially its name was 'Jayasamhita'. Later in the Gupta period it was named 'Mahabharata'. Paramgyaani Vyas ji allowed everyone to read the Mahabharata, it is clear that his vision has been universal.

The basic concept of Indian philosophy is Sarve Bhavantu Sukhanah Sarve Santu Niramaya Sarve Bhadrani Pashayantu Ma Kashchit Bhagbhavanta.

It is believed that when a child is born in the mother's womb, emphasis is laid on taking special care of the pregnant woman, she is directed to read and listen to good anecdotes.

It is also said that when great souls are born, nature also gives indications in its own way. Vinayak started the story of Rama's birth to Vandana.

Whenever there is a loss of Dharam. Baadhi asura, lowly arrogant.

Unethical things did not come. Sitahim vipra dhenu sur dharani.

Then then the Lord has various bodies. Harhim Kripanidhi Sajjan Pir.

This chaupai is from the Balkand of Sant Tulsi Kriti Ram Charit Manas, related to the faith of Hindus. Lord Shankar is narrating to Mother Parvati. Vandana said very kindly. "I read many texts on Rama. Such as Valmiki's work Ramayana, Uttarramacharitram, Ramachandrika (Keshava), Saket Maithilisharangupta, Vanyam Raksham (Acharya Chatursen) Criticism of Vindi Nigora Ramayana Shivakumar Mishra (the travails of Tulsi Samaj) Apart from this, many commentators on Rama are interpreters.

Interrupting Vinayak said, "I am telling a beautiful story or you."

Vandana acted smilingly and said, "That is the only question and answer in my beloved Ram Katha."

"I end this story. Don't you want to hear my story?

Papa's orders have to be obeyed, that's why I am saying it.

"Listen further sir, Kamil Bulke (Belgium) Siddha and Purush Ram Sukhdas, Dr. Narendra Kohli, Amish Tripathi, besides this many people have thrown light about Ram."

     SACRIFICED LIFE

Vinayak said, "Enough, shut your mouth, I feel easy."

"So now I say you have to listen?"

"Siddha Purush Ram Kinkar ji, Bapu Murari, Awadheshanand Giri, Sadhvi Ma Amrita etc., who have discoursed and explained on Ram, are guilty of selling the name of Ram and degrading the character of the society by deceiving the country. There is a punishment for their crime.

The taste of Amritmayras of Ram Katha kept going. Suspicion, disbelief, reasoning, some such situation has arisen - in place of love, affection, surrender, ego has taken it, meanwhile the light has gone out. The mood of both changed and in the arrangement of lighting, both of them operated the inverter. It happened again in the light room, but now the joy of listening to the story kept on going. How did the time pass at 12 o'clock in the night?

Vinayak and Vandana started trying to sleep. When thoughts start rising in the mind and change at such a rapid pace which is not controlled by the person, he tries to sleep but cannot sleep. There would be a turmoil of thoughts that did not seem to end. For specific information about the story of Rama, he turned his attention to the psychic penetrating Veda Tripathi.

Who is Ved Tripathi? Vandana, woke up in the morning of nectar, remembered in the morning

Karaagre vasate lakshmee karamadhye sarasvatee.

Karamoole sthito brahma prabhaate kar darshanam.

After seeing both his hands, she touched the earth and bowed down.

Sarvamangalmagalye shive sarvarthasadhike.

Sharanye Tryambake Gauri Narayani Namostute.

She came into the courtyard, looked at the mirror, smiled, and went to the bathroom. After taking a bath, she went to the kitchen to make tea.

It was 6 o'clock. Vinayak was still sleeping. Vandana did not think it appropriate to wake him up. Thinking about the night and smiling inside at his annoyance would be happy - " How did I close his mouth. "

She went to the room where he was sleeping, seeing him, she said, "Raja sahib, wake up, it was 6 o'clock in the morning." Hearing this, Vinayak turned his side and said, "Darling, let me sleep."

Vandana then splashed cold water on his face.

Because of this, he immediately got up and started murmuring,

"What is it? What is it?"

"Tea is ready, come to the kitchen and take it."

"Please give it here."

"If you want to come here, take it, I went to worship."

"The husband is God, the worship of the husband is the religion of the wife."

"First be truthful, quit joking, get up."

Vinayak got up quickly, he brushed. Standing in front of the mirror smiled and then called out loudly, "Ma'am where is my tea?"

The answer came from the worship room, "Take it on the kitchen platform, if it has become cold, then heat it on the gas. Now let me take the pooja."

After worship, Vandana went to the kitchen. Prepared food. She prepared two tiffins one for Vinayak, one for himself. It is common to quarrel with each other. Both kept trying to prove their superiority.

Vinayak was working as a clerk in the court and Vandana was a teacher in the council school. Vinayak was a carefree cool man. It became common practice to come home late because of the nomadic nature. It is never taken into account whether there is flour in the house or not, whether there is vegetable or not. Vandana takes full care of the house

Ved Tripathi is a senior advocate, all his children are well settled. Two girls are abroad. A boy Yash is a professor in IIT Guwahati.

Ved Tripathi is established as a reputed advocate. But now he does limited work, his junior Lakshmi looks after the work from court to home. It is Lakshmi who maintains the court files.

There is a routine of Veda Tripathi. Waking up at Amrit Bela, then going to Nirala Park for Morning Walk. Coming back home after spending happy time with the people, then going to the lunch break at 11 o'clock, working in the court till 01 o'clock, then drinking tea in the Bajpayee canteen and giving tea to those who come in contact with him and the audience of his Ram-Katha, Afternoon - Telling Ram Katha from 02 to 03 PM. Veda Tripathi has a special study of religious texts. In this way, he has also been a Hindi literature master and research student.

Ved Tripathi recites Ram-Katha in Nirala Park every day, the audience of his Ram-Katha first from 01 to 01.30 afternoon, after drinking free tea, it is the daily rule to listen to the story from 02 to 02.45.

Vinay used to narrate the story of Rama to Vandana every night, as per the orders of his father Bhishma Narayan.

He used to narrate Ram Katha, but the style of telling Ram Katha was not attractive, due to which the story did not get interesting and he did not even have knowledge of many episodes of Ram Katha, that is why he got his name written in the audience of Ved Tripathi's Ram Katha. He also started enjoying free tea, free Ram Katha. By the way, there is a tradition, there is a religious system - there is a provision to give dakshina to the audience for listening to the story of Rama.

At 01 o'clock in the day, the audience of Ram Katha would come to Bajpayee canteen to drink free tea of Ved Bhai, followed by sachets of water and tea, which would reach Nirala Park by 2 o'clock in the day while joking with each other. Nirala Park is built in the roundabout. In the middle of the park is the statue of Pandit Suryakant Tripathi 'Nirala', adjacent to it is a circular tank with water fountains. It feels so good when water runs in those fountains. The East South Pond is circular, around which there is a path with railings, through which people come and go in the park. To the north of the park there are many facilities for children to exercise with play material. There are soft soft green grass and systematically planted palm trees. Two sitting platforms covered by three sheds, cement benches for the people are lying all over the park in which people sit.

The seating area in the park is very picturesque. After the east way from the pond, four cement benches are made in a rectangular form, there is such a gap between those benches that two men can come together. There are 6 trees around the rectangular benches which provide shade. On the other hand, Ved Tripathi narrates Ram Katha by sitting on a long cement bench facing west and north-south. People of all caste communities come there to listen to the story of Ram. Among the scholars, lawyers, doctors, scribes, teachers, students, ignorant small and big people, etc.

In order to narrate the story to Vinayak Vandana, he would listen very carefully to the story of Ved Tripathi, ask questions in between, and tell the same story to him at night. It is a belief that if a pregnant woman listens to the story of a great man, her qualities come in the child born in her womb.

There is an incident in Mahabharata – Arjuna told the story of breaking the Chakravyuh to Subhadra. Subhadra gave birth to Abhimanyu. The same Abhimanyu got trapped in the Chakravyuh and was killed by deceit.

Concerns

There are moments in the life of every human being when he has to find the answer himself. The answers may be right or wrong. It is very difficult to come out of a state of conflict. Some people commit suicide when they do not know any option. In such a transition period, there is a search for light. Ideological differences are natural in the family, in the country, in the country and in the world, but decisions have to be taken keeping in mind the circumstances of the country from time to time.

Bhishmanarayan Sharma's life has been full of struggle and today he is established as an eminent lawyer. There is a dispute in his family whether Partha should be sent to the Defence or not. The whole family is on one side, Sharma Ji is on the other. He is simple in nature but sometimes he becomes so stubborn, fighting till the last moment to implement his definite idea. Partha is working as a computer engineer in the American company Blue Sky with a package of 80 lakhs. His age is only 24 years. Being sharp-minded, he achieved great success in a short time.

In the family Vinayak, Vinita, Kaushalya, Arjun were all against sending Partha to Defence, their own reasoning was that leaving such a huge package of 80 lakhs and going to the Defence department is ridiculous, it has all the facilities. What would he do by becoming a lieutenant captain? Left-right will do. Yes sir, salute sir will do. These things were bothering Sharma ji. Everyone is saying that Sharma Ji is a crack mind. Neither himself lives in peace nor does he allow it to remain.

Vinita, Vinayak, and Kaushalya who are Partha's mother, father, and grandmother were sitting on the same sofa in the room. On the other hand, Sharma Ji was sitting on a comfortable chair. It was 11 o'clock in the night. It was the month of December. The winter was enough. Everyone wore winter clothes.

Kaushalya said with anguish, "You know the story of Dr. Bharadwaj's son?

Listen, Partha is my dearly beloved grandson, I cannot deliberately put him to death. At this time the threat of war is looming. When will the war start?

In between Vinayak agreed with Kaushalya and said- "Iran and America are in a way like war, they are harming each other. Terrorism is at its peak. Soldiers are being killed every day,

And you have set the tune of sending Partha to the military, how are you, Baba? You say I love him, I love him very much. ,

Sharma Ji said raising his hand in passion - "Just enough he will go to the Defence".

The atmosphere got very hot. Vinita said in very polite, restrained words - "Ask Partha also"

Kaushalya Dadi said, "That incompetent will never deny the words of his Baba, I narrate the story of Dr. Bhardwaj, listen to Partha's Mundh Buddhi Baba."

From today, 30 years ago we used to live in Kanpur Chowk. There was such a thing that there was contact with the high-level people of elite families, some of them were doctors and their families. Dr. Bhalla's wife Surekha was my close friend. She was very fat. Once she came to our house, we used to live in a three-story house. The stairs of that house were narrow, she got stuck in it. Well, somehow she came out in a slanting position. She used to talk and gossip. She did not have any children, that's why she always remained in the sorrow and happiness of others, there was a lot of respect in the society, she used to help the poor helpless people.

Grandmother further said while increasing her point-

The husband of the woman working in our house used to be ill, he did not have money for his treatment. Her husband had a heart-related disease, the treatment of which was very expensive. When I told Mrs. Dr. Bhalla in this regard, she said "I will get a letter written from Dr. Saheb, you take it and show it to Dr. Bharadwaj, he will do the free treatment."

To this, I said "Your husband is also a great doctor. Why can't he cure it?"

He explained to me "My husband is a physician. Dr. Bhardwaj is a heart specialist. He gives free treatment and he is a great devotee, a saint in a way."

Small and big events that happen in life change human life. Some such incidents happened in the life of Gautam Buddha also. He became

Tathagata. Although he did not believe in the existence of God, and the soul

But propounded the doctrine of karma. In Hindu Sanatan tradition, they are accepted as an incarnation of Vishnu.

Mrs. Surekha Bhalla took Kaushalya's hand in her hand and said very intimately - "Dr. Bhardwaj is a god messenger, treating his patients with great devotion like worship - meditating in the morning and doing charity. Would doctors from abroad also consult him?"

It is also necessary to mention here Baba i.e. Sai Baba. She became emotional while speaking. And asked for water.

Kaushalya herself brought water in the glass and indicated to the maid to make tea. After some time she drank water before tea and became normal then she started his life again.

Baba says- "The hands of service are more important than the lips of worship. There are two big doctors in the hospital built in Putta Parthi like Dr. Trehan, Dr. CP Singh, Dr. Jain, Dr. Maqsood Ansari, Dr. Ramesh Trivedi, Dr. Robert, etc give free to visit one day in their hospital.

Kaushalya said- "Where were you talking about Dr. Bhardwaj right now? Are you talking about Sai Baba now?"

"Yes, I was saying this, Dr. Bhardwaj's treatment was expensive and only rich people could afford it. Suddenly an incident changed his life." She had been saying her words for an hour. Kaushalya's curiosity kept increasing.

"Dr. Bhardwaj's only son was Ram Bhardwaj, he was fast in studies, he did M.Sc. Physics in first-class from D.A.V College, Kanpur. He applied for the post of pilot in the Air Force, he got selected. Most of all he was congratulated, everything was fine. But then in the medical test, he was unfit. Something was not understood. This made Ram Bhardwaj a big upset. "

Mrs. Bhardwaj said, "All right. Well, he should stay here and look after us."

Dr. Bhardwaj was thinking about Ram's career. He said to Ram "For medical means take time for your next Check-Up, you will improve and ok in it."

Ram said- "Hey father, what should I tell? Now nothing will happen to me."

Meanwhile, a call came from South India - it was an urgent call. Somebody was looking for time to show the serious critical patient. Immediately Dr. Bhardwaj made the appointment.

Dr. Bhardwaj immediately reached the hospital. Patient Ramanathan was brought by his parents by air.

Dr. Bhardwaj did a quick Check Up. The patient was sent to the emergency room. Treatment started.

His father said, "Sir, I have deposited the fees."

"Ok." Dr. Bhardwaj said "You have come on time, if you were late, it would have been very difficult,"

His father and mother said - "Doctor sir - will it be okay?"

"It will be 100% fine guaranteed God bless you By the grace of God, his health started improving rapidly. ."

He recovered completely after fifteen days of treatment.

Dr. Bhardwaj had to do a heart operation. The operation lasted seven hours. being successful.

Before the heart operation, the patient's family members had to take a class. Instructions are given on how to take care of the patient and all the precautions for the operation are given. Giving medicines etc. The medical expenses came to around 15 lakhs. He made 10 lakh donuts separately to the hospital.

After that, suddenly one day, Dr. Bhardwaj got a call from a Rashtrapati Bhavan - "Your Excellency the President wants to meet you."

What could be a happier moment for a doctor? His work was appreciated. Dr. Bhardwaj became very happy.

The arrival date has been fixed. Government alert. Police officers, collectors, and other officials contacted Dr. Bhardwaj.

Dr. hosted a banquet in honor of the President, along with officers of the administration and Defence department. Very pleasant atmosphere After dinner, in solitude, the President expressed his gratitude and said that "You have treated and cured my son-in-law, I will always be indebted. If there is any service worthy of me, then tell me."

Dr. Bhardwaj said without hesitation- "My son Ram Bhardwaj has passed the examination for the post of pilot in the Air Force but has made him unfit in medical, whatever the reason."

It is necessary to say here that it is a good thing to choose the right officers and it is necessary but sometimes some officers themselves create some unnecessary situation for the sake of economic benefits, due to which they have to oblige them even if there are suitable capable candidates.

His Excellency the President immediately gave some instructions to his secretary. It did not take long to understand him immediately. "Your son will surely become a successful Air Force officer," said His Excellency.

Dr. Bhardwaj called his son. He asked the signal to touch His Majesty's feet

He touched his feet, he blessed him by placing his hand on his head. "May you be successful! God Bless You."

Mrs. Surekha Bhalla was telling the story, she again requested Kaushalya to have tea. After drinking tea again, saying 'Jai Sai Ram' started describing the incident further. Kaushalya was also enjoying listening to the story. It was eight o'clock in the night. The driver entered the room and said, "Madam, how long will it take? I was told by the doctor, to come by seven o'clock, it is seven o'clock."

Kaushalya gave him the cup of tea, he refused by nodding his head, but at the behest of Surekha, took tea and went out of the room and started drinking. After a while, he said again - "Madam what is your order?"

"I'll leave for a while." hearing this, he went out.

Surekha said, "The next incident is very heart-wrenching. Two days after His Excellency's departure, Dr. Bhardwaj got the appointment of Ram Bhardwaj, in which he was ordered to report for training by March 1.

Ram Bharadwaj was getting marriage proposals but due to some term condition, he could not get married for two years. For this reason, the marriage proposals were postponed.

Ram Bhardwaj joined the training. After two years of training, he became a commissioned officer. Well dressed he came home after two years. The parents were very happy. They distributed sweets in the colony. Everyone started coming to congratulate him. His Excellency the President himself congratulated and again expressed his gratitude. His son-in-law Ramanathan came for a routine Check-Up. Doctor Bharadwaj kept him in his house and gave him love like his own son. He became, in a way, part of the family. When he started leaving after the routine Check Up, he was given full respect as a son-in-law.

When he started going back, the husband and wife gave him cheques of one lakh as a gift, he rejected those cheques, So, expressing authority, Mrs. Bharadwaj, while turning her hand with love on her back, said – "Now she is older than her mother."

Ram Bharadwaj went to drop him at the airport in his car. We all complement each other.

Being bored after hearing such a long story, Bhishma Narayan Sharma while addressing Kaushalya said - "Partner! Just let your story be heard. Now stop this story and now it is decided that Parth has to go to Defence Service, the country needs him."

Kaushalya said in a loud voice in a fit of rage, "I am not finished yet."

"Your story has become the story of Alif Laila which will never end."

"He who listens to an incomplete talk never reaches the right conclusion. Partha will not go to the Defence Department. Will not go. I have said this, then these are my last words."

"Hey dad, let mom's talk be complete. The daughter-in-law said- "You guys are fighting like junior class students."

Bhishma's anger increased and said "Shut your mouth"

Indians have a habit of speaking in English when they were angry, now their anger was touching the seventh sky.

Meanwhile, Sharma Ji gave a cup of tea to Kaushalya. He reluctantly took the cup of tea. But after a while, the tea changed the mood very well.

This time Kaushalya said very seriously - listen to what happened next, she again started adding a link to the story told in the past.

Meanwhile, Sharma Ji smiled and said- "Dada Wala's way of telling your story. Dada meant Kaushalya's father. He used to say anything, in the meantime, after doing some work, he would start talking from there, where The statement used to be missing from them, this is also the specialty of the person. Some people forget where what we were saying.

Kaushalya again started saying "Ram Bhardwaj got posting. Ram Bhardwaj had to go to the USA with some important people from Captain's Boeing 3S Classic. It was a secret mission. But such an untoward incident happened in the air. The air crashed and the ship fell into the sea. Pilot Sahib all the passengers went to the lap of death. How all this happened, no one knows anything. Giving importance to this incident, all the leading newspapers were published.

Commission Inquiry, Commission of Inquiry was set up whose points were: Air crash caused by the enemy country attack, due to lack of technology in the aircraft, ignoring adequate measurement penalty in the purchase of aircraft and why the aircraft lost contact with radar? It all became a matter of deliberation.

Simply, Dr. Bhardwaj's heart was broken by this tragic incident. Initially, Dr. Bhardwaj could not believe this incident. But when he was convinced, his sons were ready to commit suicide in mourning. He was saying over and over again "There is nothing left in my life now. My life is meaningless now."

Seeing his condition, people would have remembered the episode of Ayodhya Kand Ramcharit Manas of King Dasharatha.

His doctor companion explained that the enjoyment of birth and death, happiness, loss, loss-benefit-separation of loved ones, all these times keep on getting ruined like night and day under karma.

Foolish people rejoice in happiness and weep in sorrow. But those who are patient consider both of them equal in their mind. According to religious beliefs, the given arrangements have to be followed. That is why rituals have been arranged on a psychological basis.

Dr. Bhardwaj had gone completely mad in his son's mourning, he was not even eating food. When Dr. Bhardwaj was sitting alone after the ritual, his mind was sad. Remembering the son, suddenly tears started filling in his eyes. Then suddenly he felt the sweet sound of Lord Krishna in his ears and he felt as if Lord Krishna was smiling and saying to him, "You have been born for the welfare of the people. You are using your ability and ability through the medical profession. Put it in public service, your son will definitely come back."

After hearing this, as if suddenly his samadhi broke down. Simply, from that day onwards Dr. Bhardwaj treats patients free of cost, he is a deity.

Dr. Bhalla's wife Surekha ends her talk here. She gave a recommendation letter sent by Dr. Bhalla to Dr. Bhardwaj.

Kaushalya further said, "That's why I am against sending Partha to Defence. You love him the most. Will you still send him?"

There was complete silence in the atmosphere. Everyone became silent, no one was talking to each other. A stuffy hall.

Bhishma Narayan Sharma wanted to say something, wanted to present his statement with logic, but he did not do anything. He went quietly to his bedroom.

It was one o'clock in the night. The whole family was sleeping. Were considering the danger looming on the world stage. Political parties also make deals for the country for their personal interest. If he saves the country, then he is the true soldier of the country, considering all these things, wrote a letter to his family, also endorsed a copy of it to Partha. No one knows what is written in the letter, it is just that how to save the nation.

Resolution Letter

Letter writing is a type of art. Scientific advancement has established its influence in every field. Human life has become more convenient than before due to new inventions. The subject to be considered here is that when and how much to use new technology. In the meantime, the robot was created. Artificial intelligence has developed, in this competition, competition is going on in the countries of the world.

Making an atom bomb is science, but when to use it is philosophy - sometimes we talk of peace and sometimes of war. The world is full of complications. Sometimes a person has to sacrifice personal selfishness for a bigger purpose.

Once upon a time, pigeons work as postmen, even interesting statements come, love letters were exchanged in many secret ways. To allow the pleasure of reading love letters in solitude. Wife used to write letters to her husband, lover to his girlfriend, son to his parents and family members. Asking the postman due to the delay in the arrival of the letter - "Brother, did the letter come or not?" Then came the time for the telephone trunk. Then this country became Digital India. Where the digital world was created, the same cybercrime has taken birth. When a law is made, its breakers are born.

Meetings of government administration and executives of big companies have started through video conferencing. Oral evidence is also being recorded in the court through video conferencing. Today's man has become a machine. Sensations are moving towards emptiness, what will be the time to come is a considerable question.

It is one o'clock in the night, there is silence all around, I was sitting in my room, writing a letter to the family in the present context.

<u>Letter</u>

My beloved

Many blessings

Man is a slave of circumstances. Everything is nature-born, but here I will not explain Sankhya Yoga, Karma Yoga, and Bhakta Yoga. Simply saying this with positive thinking from common sense paves the right path.

Suicide has been termed as a sin in Indian philosophy. Many institutions have their own views in the situational environment. Suicide comes under the category of sin.

From today, 45 years ago when I was a student of D.A.V. degree college, Shri Prakash Tiwari, Jai Prakash Trivedi, N. Mathani, Udayshankar Awasthi, Ramesh Bhatia Mohd. Naseem etc. were among my class friends. We used to tell each other about our condition, laugh and joke, have fun. Sometimes we used to talk nonsense that was baseless. Yes, Ramakrishna, senior to us, was also one of them. He was the topper. He used to tell good things to us, we used to take his jokes every once in a while, one name was Babulal Shukla. We were just ordinary class students. There were students of the third and second divisions, but everyone had their own dreams. Some belonged to a wealthy family, and some belonged to a poor family. Dayashankar Pandey studied in Christ Church Degree College.

We all would sometimes bunk a class when a new picture was shown in the picture hall. We used to sit in the back seat in class. Then we would disappear from class as soon as we said 'yes sir' to the attendees. Sometimes some professors used to even catch them.

One important thing about the college was that of Pandit Vidya Dhar Sharma. He was the head clerk but his status was more than that of the principal. He was of normal stature, fair complexion, healthy, possessed an attractive personality. His voice had impressive magical power. He used to scold, punish the students for their arrogance, but later also forgave them. The entire operation of the Maha Vidyalaya was in the hands of Sharma Ji. The students used to escape from his sight. The college was a kind of factory. It used to run from 6 in the morning till 9 in the night. Law classes were held in the evening shift.

This college of Kanpur metropolis was unique in itself. In our time, schools were known as Principals, as for example D.A. V Inter College Scholar Respected Shivkumar Lal Srivastava, B. N. s. D. Putti Lal Ji, G. N. NS. Inter College Shri Hardwari Lal Tandon, Marwari College was famous by the name of Satguru Sharan Awasthi. Similarly, degree colleges were famous due to the names of professors and principals of special qualifications. I am not able to give the names of all the teachers here, so I am writing whatever I remember.

A name is taken with great respect Dr. Madan Mohan Pandey, who was a professor of Political Science, his lectures were attended by renowned professors. Former Prime Minister Atal Bihari was also his student.

Dr. Munshi Ram Sharma in Hindi, Som Siddhanath Mishra, Dr. Kamath in English, and Dr. Saxena Devi Shankar Awasthi was famous, who were rich in special talent. Pandit Siddha Nath Mishra did only M.A. But he got many students to do research work.

Under him, many students did Ph.D. At Halim Muslim Degree College, M. Rizvi Sahib was the principal. He kept an eye on all the students. Let me mention one incident. Normally Hindu-Muslim fights take place, so it is discussed.

It was the month of Ramadan. I had submitted my fee waiver application. I was going through financial difficulties. I told Professor Dr. D.K. Mishra "Sir please forgive my fee."

He said "You go straight to Rizvi sahib and speak your mind"

I did the same. I went to the principal room with permission. "Sir I came in sir." Seeing me standing at the door, he called me by hand gesture.

Rizvi sir heard me, waived my full fee and said "If you want books then tell" then asked "Are there any other difficulties?" There was a sweetness in his voice. There Dr. Khan was from English, Bal Govind Gupta in Hindi, Dr. Kaushik in Arthashastra. I can't remember a name, but I have never seen such a professor in history in the world. He used to write notes on history without a book. He had a master's degree in European History. What he taught, he imprinted in the minds of his students in their minds.

Inter College teachers like Munilal Mishra Munidra, Gyandev Agnihotri, Dr. R. D. Tripathi, Devendra Nath Pandey Shastri, Omkarnath Mehrotra, Dr. S. N. Pandey, etc. were also blessed with a special idol whose name I take with great respect.

When I was studying in class 9 in G.N.K. Inter College. Dr. S. N. Pandey was a research student, he studied Hindi. After that, he went to D.B.S. Degree College. He was counted among the most influential people. His physical fitness was visible. Fair complexion, chubby, moving like an elephant, eloquent speech. He was honored not only by the state government but even by the central government, he was decorated with the Padma Shri award. He did research work on the poetic practice of Meera, a devotee of Lord Krishna Murli Manohar.

Hindi Pracharini Samiti was established by my revered Gurudev Padma Shri Dr. Shyam Narayan Pandey on January 10, 1966. The idea of establishing the institution belonged to him and the naming was also done by him. Dr. Pandey used to take great care of his disciples and also used to promote them. Arrogant nature fearless was rich in special talent. An era of Kanpur literary consciousness is called Dr. Shyamnarayan Pandey.

That era is said to be of Dr. Shyam Narayan Pandey. He had many disciples. One of those names comes from Dr. Maheshchandra Mishra (Vidhu). Instead of Vidhu, he was called Chandramaj from Dular. Shyam Narayan Pandey had great affection for him. Dr. Vidhu wrote a book on him that was published.

Dr. Surya Prasad Shukla, Dr. R. D. Awasthi, Seva Vatsyayan, Upendra Shastri, etc. are still remembered as milestones in the period of their time. Overall, Kanpur has hidden many secrets in its womb. From time to time, humans penned on various subjects. There is no justification to write all this in the letter, but without the role, the novel seems incomplete.

Our fellow members were of different nature. Ramesh Bhatia belonged to a good family and used to laugh and joke a lot in conversation. I remember an incident from that time, one day, the girl's brother came to talk about the marriage of one of our companions. Our friend asked his name-

On being named by him, everyone included him in their conversation. Then one of our colleagues Ramesh Bhatia commenting on the institution of marriage said that "Fresh milk available in the market, then what the use of saving the calf ?" The girl's brother went away after hearing this and went home and narrated the story of us loafer people, after which the girl's father came and we were all given bitter medicine for the preaching. Our life was passing days in the fun without any systematic planning work.

Time keeps on educating the person from time to time, it is just a matter of understanding him. It is believed that Lord Rama carries Kaal's bow and arrows in his lotus feet. Different religions have done the science of division of time according to their laws. Nanosecond, minute, hour, day-night, month, year, etc., and so on, the time is taken by the Sun to complete one zodiac, is called a solar month. There is a year outside the solar months, which according to the Surya Siddhanta is of 365 days, 15 hours, 31 moments, and 30 pipals. The description of Satya Yuga, Treta, Dwapara and Kali Yuga is that in each era, great souls made the place of birth holy. Time is the truth, only in the present person's life. He dies neither in the past nor in the future, this is the truth of life only in the present.

Ramesh Bhatia was a first-year B.Sc. student, he failed in the first year itself, so he became sad. Out of self-guilt, he decided to commit suicide. Suicide is a crime. In a landmark judgment on 9 March 2015, the Supreme Court granted the legal right of passive euthanasia to a person suffering from cerebrovascular disease. Article 21 of the Indian Constitution gives the right to live with dignity and to die with dignity.

The idea of committing suicide is said to be the mental weakness of the person.

Ramesh Bhatia, being a friend to me, spoke his heart, although at that time I was also going through some such situation because I too failed. But to prove myself more intelligent, I gave a vigorous lecture. I had read the life story of many great people. In it, a poet was going to commit suicide out of frustration with life. At the same time, some children were collectively reading the composition of that poet, he became conscious after listening to his composition, he left the thought of suicide and moved towards his set goal. It is time that creates such a coincidence.

I told Ramesh Bhatia "Dude why don't you apply for a short service commission? I am also applying. The qualification is inter science (from maths), which you have. Changed his mind, he applied in inter science, his I got selected but I didn't.

He retired as a lieutenant colonel, later he opened his own academy. It was the result of his dedication and hard work.

Sometimes we have to think that the country needs us and we have to give our services to the country. People are not able to do big things in their life. Whenever there is a crisis in the country, then the whole country stands united. The same situation happened in 1962 during the Sino-India war. In an emergency situation, the government has to act with great prudence.

In the Second World War, Churchill, at his discretion, saved the people of Britain from Hitler's fighting skills. He saved the public from blackouts and other precautions.

I will say this much, self-confidence protects the society and the country by giving good thoughts to the person. A soldier ran away from the army. He started farming at home. The fear of going to the border in the war fascinated him with life. Army officials issued a warrant against him. When he came to know that an army officer had come to his house, he hid in a store used to store straw, where he was bitten by a snake and died prematurely. A person can die anywhere. Running away from duty is death.

Partha did research work on cybercrime with an in-depth study of information technology software and hardware. He was so genius that he is called a supercomputer. You. s. The company had contracted him for two years. All facilities, good package, and air tour. The Government of India also made an offer but did not react.

There is an incident, Dr. A. K Kothari did research on quantum theory. His research work was appreciated globally but he could not get the professor post at Himachal University because most of the appointments here are on the basis of recommendation and money. Dr. Kothari went to America when his research work came to the fore, the Indian government called but did not want to come due to frustration but still, he had a love for his country.

In the end, I extend my heartfelt blessings to all, may the omnipresent God bless everyone with happiness and prosperity. I don't have any pressure.

Partha is free to choose his career at his own discretion. I don't want to impose my wishes on anyone. Wherever you live, you must preserve your family Sanatani Sanskars. Time is the teacher who teaches a person.

The nation is paramount. Responsible for self, family, society, province, and country. In all of these, the nation is paramount, must consider this point.

With the wish of all-around development, I end the letter here.

Always yours
Bhishmanarayan Sharma

Varsha, Varun and Vinay had been together in their student life. Varun and Varsha's love for each other was not hidden from anyone. It had become second nature for them to consult each other in difficult situations. Vinay knew that Varun used to be absorbed in thoughts of Varhsa. He liked being near Varsha and talking to her. The purpose of student life is to pay attention to one's studies and to pass examinations with good marks but often students get entangled in love affairs and spoil their careers.

The seed of love was sown on the day when Varsha was standing in line to submit the form for M.A. Hindi Previous. Varun was standing in the other line waiting to submit his form for the M.Sc. Previous course. A girl accidentally pushed Varsha and her form went flying out of her hands; but before it could land in a pool of mud, Varun managed to jump and catch it in his hands. Some 'sorries' and a few angry words were exchanged, but thankfully the form had been saved The time for submitting the forms was coming to an end; Varun looked at the form briefly and returned it to Varsha.

　　SACRIFICED LIFE

She did not say thank you but looked at him gratefully. Showing sympathy, Varun offered to submit the form, when Vinay appeared and asked him if he could help. Varun gave him the form and asked him to submit it without losing any time. Vinay did not deposit it at the counter, but went inside the room and submitted it.

Varsha had not paid the application fees so she paid it to Vinay and they got acquainted.

Varun decided that all three of them would sit in the canteen and have tea and he would submit his form the next day. He paid for all three of them and thus the first day of college came to an end. Varun had decided that he would also do Hindi M.A. and told this to Vinay. Vinay warned him that his father would not take this decision lightly since it would not fetch Varun a job, but Varun was adamant.

Education in our country is nothing more than a stepping stone to getting a job. Policies are framed and changed accordingly, but Varun's objective was a bit different.

Varsha was extremely attractive. Her body was as supple as a person used to doing regular exercise; her face was full and she had large eyes and when she smiled a dimple appeared in her cheek.

Beauty does not have a fixed definition; it depends on the beholder. Beauty means attractiveness. It is that which appeals to your senses. Varun fell for Varsha's allure.

He took admission in Hindi M.A. despite all appeals to the contrary. The admission was enabled due to the acceptance of the head of the department- Dr. L.K. Pandey. There are some professors who manage to create an interest in the minds of their students towards their subject. Kalyan Chaube was a textile engineer in B.A.C. Red Tamarind Textiles and received a decent salary and had been allotted a house to live in. It was Pandey ji's aim to make a special place for Hindi in the global arena and wanted that marking in examinations should be lenient, but there were many people who were against this.

Varun had never imagined that he would one day be enrolled in Hindi M.A. classes. But here he was pursuing it-with Varsha as his classmate. They soon started going out and hanging out together.

The time was three noon. Dr. Panday was taking a class in room no 14 40 on the first floor of the building. There must have been about 25 students in the class. The fan was whirring at a speed of '2', since the weather was quite pleasant and it was raining outside. The rain was coming in gusts and the scenery outside the window was captivating. Varsha was enjoying it from her seat near the window. Varun was sitting on the first seat of the second row from where he did not have a clear view of Varsha, but could clearly see everything in the glass because the lights had been switched on since it had become quite dark. Varun was busy looking at Varsha's reflection in the glass.

Dr. Panday was explaining the poetic analysis of Agyey composed by Sacchidanad Hiranand Vatsayan. Agyey has given a new direction and status to Hindi literature. He has given a new style, new analogy and new language to Hindi poetry. His thoughts pertaining to poetry can be found in his poetry collection and essays. It was his belief that art can be created only when an artist is unable to prove his social usefulness and becomes sad and becomes steeped in his loneliness. In his own words- 'Our imagined weak bodies have believed that it is difficult to participate in the imaginary society and become habitual to the feeling of uselessness and made that sphere vaster by our rebellion and taught it a new usefulness- the experience of beauty'.

Dr. Panday drew the attention of his students and said, 'in the above statement of Agyey one can hear the clear echo of the Western philosopher and psychologist, Freud'.

The modern person is nothing but a lump of taboo sexual desires, his mind is loaded with sexual fantasies that have been suppressed and blunted. His sense of beauty has also been assaulted by this.

The imagination of sexual gratification in the context of art and beauty manages to sway a devotee to an extent. From physical beauty it enters into the realm of lust and is destroyed if it is restricted there, but if let loose one derives intense pleasure from it. Taking an example from Osho's book, "From sex to Samadhi" sexual pleasure and sensual experience are different from the experience of the soul and it cannot be expressed in words and its minutest details cannot be described.

All the students were lost in the lecture. Varun and Varsha listened intently but could not absorb it fully. When the bell rang, all the students left one by one.

When Varun started searching for her the next day, he found that Varsha had not come., and he could not find out the reason. Then he came to know that her father had been transferred to Aligarh and she had gone there. He received a great setback, but was helpless.

Sometimes a person becomes the victim of ire of his own family, but when he doesn't achieve what he wants, he loses control over himself and starts thinking of alternatives to leading his life. The college that he liked till yesterday, held no interest for him today. He thought of Vinay; when he went to his house he came to know that he too had been transferred to Aligarh. He thought that he would go there and find him; so he took his address and started for Aligarh.

Varsha was also attracted to Varun's physical strength and his style of talking, etc. Varun was tall and broad and had brown hair. His cheeks were slightly ruddy and hair were wavy and he looked like an Afghan Pathan.

Vinay was living in a rented house in Adarsh Nagar; Vinita was also living with him. She was doing Sanskrit M.A.. Varsha studied in the same college. Both knew each other. Varun would search for Varsha the whole day long and come back to Vinay's house at night. There was a Hanuman temple where it was a belief that whoever tied a yellow-red-blue thread on an iron rod, his prayer would be heeded. Varun did not believe these superstitions, but still tied a thread to the rod on Tuesday. There are many such places where people perform such rites and their wishes are granted. There is no scientific reason for this, but the theory of faith is accepted.

A peculiar incident occurred. Varsha and Vinay lived in the same locality. After the row of houses there was an intersection where traffic never stopped. On one side were the Hindu inhabitants and on the other side were the Pakistanis. There was a Hindu-Muslim riot and the situation became tense.

Varun was walking fearlessly through the Muslim area. He was unaware of the divide, but since he was looking like a Pathani, the Muslims did not say anything. As soon as he entered the Hindu area, some Hindu youth surrounded him thinking that he was a Muslim and gave him a slap. Varun was taken aback.

'I am a Hindu.'

'Tell us your correct name.'

Before he could tell his name he was pushed.

'Ok...if you are a Hindu, show your 'janeyu'

'He is not wearing a 'janeyu'

'He is a Muslim.'

A middle aged man said, "Recite the Gaytri Mantra".

"Ok...leave it, read the Hanuman Chalisa"

Varun got so flustered, he could not remember anything.

There was no symbol of Hindutva on his body

In the end they said, "Recite the RamCharitManas."

Then somebody said, 'He cannot do that also'.

'He is a Muslim.'

Varun was quietly standing there-not grasping anything.

On the other side of the road were three girls and a middle-aged man who pointed out and said, "Look what's happening." One of the girls ran swiftly(the people knew her since she was a local) and called out loudly, "HE is a Hindu, a Hindu!"

Everyone turned towards the girl and stopped beating Varun. When she reached closer, one of them asked her, "Do you know him?"

Breathing hard, she replied, "Arre! He is Varun Dixit, he has been my classmate in DAV college, Kanpur.

Everyone was shocked and gave him water to drink. The crowd gradually dispersed and the police came.

There was a police inspector along with some constables. Varun was questioned. Varsha told them that things were fine and an accident had been averted.

Suddenly, the matter became heated. A drama used to be enacted in Agra University. The writer was a famous personality of the movie world-Gyan Dev Agnihotri. It contained a message on Hindu-Muslim unity, along with their opposing views.

There is a word-'misunderstanding'-that is a part of the human nature. There is an incident related to this. There were two brothers. One worked in theatre and the second worked elsewhere. Both lived together. Hindu-Muslim riots broke out. The brother working in the theatre had to return home after his rehearsal- he put on a Muslim style beard and came out from the Muslim colony. He knocked at the door of his house; his brother peeped from inside and seeing that it was a Muslim person, stabbed him with a knife. The brother asked him what he ahd done. On recognizing his voice, there was wailing in the house. Such incidents also happen. This shows how the environment affects us and compels us to take action accordingly. One ends up harming one's own self or kin and this complex riddle needs to be resolved.

There is another facet to this. A Hindu Brahman Pujari saved a Muslim boy and a Muslim fakir saved a Hindu boy. Later both had to face ostracism from their own religions.

It is here that pleasure has been described. When a person feels love, he feels a different type of feeling and he wants to sustain it as long as possible. The pleasure of the 'soul' by helping others. Sometimes it has been seen that some great souls have gone through a lot of pains-even to the extent of having given their lives for others, like Jesus Christ, Socrates, Dhadichi, etc. Their sacrifice is still etched on human minds.

Vinay and Varun were nephew and Uncle as per relationship but since they were mates at school, they used to address each other by name.

Vinay sometimes addressed Varun as 'chacha' and accordingly Varsha became his choti maa. Varsha and Vinay talked a lot and since Vinay was a good poet, Varsha liked his poems; whereas Vineeta was quite averse to poetry. She believed that writers could never be responsible householders and only God could help their progeny. Such humorous talks happened when they met.

Varsha's father was an ordinary school -teacher and a suitable match for Varsha had not yet been found. Dowry is a social ill because of which many marriages take place even when there is no compatibility between the bride and groom and later causes a lot of bitterness in their marital life. In the Hindu tradition marriage is considered an institute. In other religions it is a compromise. Vinay knew what was in Varun's mind. Varun asked Vinita for her help in arranging his marriage with Varsha and Vinita agreed to it on some conditions. Varun was ready to fulfill those conditions.

Vinita kept the proposal of Varun before Varsha's family. The issue of matching horoscopes cropped up. Vinita said that Vinay knew this art.

The next day Vinay told Vinita that according to the astrologer one should not get the horoscopes matched if the girl and boy were above 18 years of age. Varsha's family ultimately agreed to the proposal. Varun's family also agreed after some initial hiccups. Varun and Varsha got tied in holy matrimony and began their married life. Varun, Varsha, Vinay and Vinita once again came baack to Kanpur and things became normal again.

Time passed and Varsha gave birth to a girl whom they named Vanshika. Vinay and Vinita had a son whom they named Parth. Twenty years passed by. Vanshika had become an IPS officer and Parth had completed his engineering and was working in a company in USA.

Vinita refused to have any sort of physical relationship with Vinay. This continued for many days and Vinay was resenting it. He wanted to know why she was behaving in this manner.

In our country we do not talk openly about sexual matters whereas it is not so in foreign countries. There is a lot of discussion in the 'Kamasutra' about these matters. The work of Vatsyasan is world famous and one finds the description of the purpose and rules regarding sexual maters but there is no provision for its education.

In AnandParv marriage is given an important place and it has been expounded that sex is an act that is performed for the fulfillment of desires-this tradition has been given propounded in many religions. Sexual talks have been discussed by various psychologists but there is a basic difference between Indian and Western thought. Marriage is a holistic system in which one can fulfill sexual desires within a certain boundary and this theory is accepted by almost all countries. Despite Vinay's many attempts, Vinita refused to have any physical contact with him. Varsha was Formally Vinay's 'chachi' and he used to address her as such. One day Vanshika had gone out somewhere. It was around 9 o'clock at night. Vinita went to her room and lied down. Vinay went near her and started rubbing her hands, but she shook him off. Varsha's footsteps could be heard outside. She crossed the courtyard and went to her room. She sat before the dressing table and started braiding her hair. Suddenly she saw Vinay's reflection in the mirror, and called him inside. He came and leaning over he said, "Chachi, you are looking very pretty." She replied, "Your 'chacha' is not here, that's why." He said to her that Vinita was not interested in having any physical contact with him and that Varsha should try and intervene. She replied that she was ready to establish physical contact with him and embraced Vinay to her chest. A current ran through Vinay. He quietly went to his room and closed the door and lied down on the bed thinking that he had just been saved from committing a sin.

Cities of lust

Talent can bloom in the unlikeliest of places and small towns are no exception. One name is that of Jeevan Dwivedi Vaidya Raj. He cured people of high status and earned great name and fame.

At the ripe old age of 93, he was still healthy of mind and body and people came from afar to be cured from him. He was a specialist of venereal diseases and has done a lot research on the digestive process and written many books on Ayurveda. He has many good qualities but one habit that takes away from him is his 'in your face' attitude. He said the truth without sugar coating it and according to him truth is always bitter.

He cured many people of incurable diseases and gained fame.

He lived in two big L-shaped rooms. There were photos of God Krishna playing the flute adorning the wall behind where he sat with a table in front of him and two chairs and two sofas and an easy chair besides 4 other chairs and a stretcher being the other furniture.

Ayurved has been there for a longer time but people give more preference to Allopathy although there are other 'pathies' like 'Unani', 'Accupressure' and magnet therapies, etc, allopathy gives quick relief. But it is also said that there are side effects in this.

There has been a lot of progress in the field of Ayurveda in the past decades. Some companies like Himalaya Drugs, Jhandu, Dabur Badiyanath, etc came up. The demand for medicines that increased one's virility also increased. All companies started making these medicines and started advertising them, resulting in the dwindling numbers of Vaids and Hakims.

A strange case was put before the Vaidya. His lawyer friend Anand Shankar had the case of a woman who had not come since 2nd or 3rd. On enquiring, it came to be known that she was not well. What was the disease? He would have to tell in the Court. She said in an embarrassed manner that he could not reveal it. She was very beautiful but one could make out the agony she was going through. They were talking when the Vaidya suddenly appeared. The lawyer introduced her saying that she could tell the Vaidy about her illness.

He diagnosed her illness to be constipation; the lawyer was surprised at his knowledge.

The vaidy was proud of his capability and experience and promised that he would be able to cure her. He told her to take medicine for a week and then report back.

The lawyer told him to get her medical certificate made to which he agreed.

The lawyer told him the date of his case and also that the honorable district magistrate, Nirmala Pandey, had invited him to her bungalow. She would send her driver and he could go; the vaidy never went there but since it was in his interest he nodded his head.

The woman was now quite sure that she would get well. The vaidy had treated many politicians, rich businessmen and officers and these people were always eager to repay his goodness.

It was six in the evening and the vaidy was attending to his patients when the same woman turned up. The vaidy gestured for her to sit and she quietly sat down.

When her turn came the vaidy told her to wait till he saw the two remaining patients and said that he would attend to her in the end. She nodded her head and sat down again. Her fifteen year daughter was with her. The vaidy kept the register and taking out a pad he started asking questions.

Name?	—	Karuna Singh.
Age?	—	36 years.
Address?	—	Moolganj, Kanpur.
Daughter's name?	—	Archana.

After writing, he took her hand in his and checked her pulse and asked her since when she was facing the problem. She replied, "Three months." 'What treatment did you take?' She showed the prescriptions of the doctors. He asked her to show her tongue, then checked her eyes, then told her to lie down on the stretcher. She went inside and lay on the stretcher. The vaidy called out to his wife. He gave her some instructions and Karuna Singh came out and sat. The vaidy gave her some medicine and instructed his wife on how it was to be given.

The wife instructed Karuna Singh, saying that there was some cream that was to be applied in the vagina and a radish that was to be inserted. The procedure was to be repeated for three days.

She took the medicine and did as instructed.

When she got up in the morning and took out the radish from her vagina she got a lot of relief. She was 70% cured and thanked the vaidy. She used to scream during the night and now she was cured. She saw that two small creatures were clinging to the radish that she had taken out and wondered how it had happened. Her old radiance had returned and her face was glowing.

She went to the vaidy after a week. A Muslim woman in a 'burqua' was with her. After seeing all his patients, the vaidy asked Karuna, "Now, tell me." She told the vaidy that her sister Aparna had come from Iraq and her husband had been murdered there. She was suffering from many diseases. The vaidy asked her to tell him everything without embarrassment and that he would cure her.

He asked his assistant to bring tea, which he brought and kept in a tray.

The vaidy asked her to take some medicine with water and then to have tea. She did exactly as told and then he asked her to get examined. As soon as she lifted her burqua, he was entranced by her beauty. He told her that she would be cured; she should tell her entire story to him. She started telling her story that was extremely heart wrenching. She started crying piteously. Those who worked there all came and asked what the matter was. The vaidy told them all to go and they dispersed.

Her throat was hoarse. There was a call for the vaidy. He replied that he couldn't come since he was attending to a special patient who was under his treatment at that time. He told her to relate her story without concealing any little point. The lady began her story-

"I had done by B.A. I got a job at the reception desk of Landmark Hotel. I slowly learned to speak in English. I met one Arif Zaidi who was a civil engineer in Iraq. We kept meeting and one day he proposed to me. I accepted and we got married. My passport and visa were made and I went to Iraq with him. It was Ok till the office of Saddam Hussain, after that it became difficult to live there.

Saddam Hussain attacked Kuwait. The area was merged into Iraq. The American forces took under their control. The Iran Israel war had been going on for a long time. Then America attacked Iraq. The situation got out of control and became an international issue. In this manner the countries terrorist organizations started a violent sexual orgy. We were kept in camps and were sexually assaulted. She started sobbing.

The vaidy gave her water and asked her to drink tea again. She became quiet a little later and then started relating her story once again.

Nadia Murad was kidnapped by the terror organization of the Islamic State and thousands of women were made the victims of sexual assault. We were kept in camps and were tortured. On refusing physical advances were mentally tortured. Efforts made at the international level were proving ineffective. She started crying again. The 93 year- old man also got agitated while hearing her story.

Nadia Murad raised her voice against the sexual violence against Yehudi girls and she was made the Goodwill Ambassador of the United Nations in 2016.

Similarly during the Congo civil war there was sexual violence. Dr.Dennis Muk Veg was awarded the Nobel Peace prize for his struggle against sexual violence. Captain PArth of the Indian Army helped the American army with great presence of mind and freed the sexually exploited women. After this thousands of women became victims of sexual diseases and started committing suicides due to the mental trauma they suffered but statistics for this are not available.

Women and men were afflicted with HIV AIDS and other skin diseases. The WHO took steps but they were negligible.

After hearing the story the vaidy asked them to get some tests done. After the test results came he consulted his son, Dr. Kant and the treatment lasted for three months. There was a lot of improvement in her health and she became better. Disease and cure are elements of life. There are problems and there are solutions. Some situations are man-made while others are events of nature. The polluted thoughts of man produce a negative environment in the society, country and entire world, and in such a situation a new light emerges and purifies the environment.

Sexual pleasure and perversity.

Dr. Rameshwar Dwivedi the famous and well known poet read out his work from the dais that had been erected at Diggi Chowk in Banda district. It was appreciated and received a standing ovation. He is a modern poet. Referring to the Judiciary and government he began his verse,

Will you allow—

- Red light streets to operate freely
- Let our cultural values be stripped
- Of their dignity and paraded in the streets.

These lines led to quite a few questions. A bride whose face is veiled with a thin satin cloth looks beautiful while a face that is artificially made up loses its grace. It is here that the difference between natural beauty and artificial beauty shows and we enter the world of vulgarity.

Captain Parth and Professor Surendra Khanna met in this poets' conference. When the professor got up to leave after the conference was over, a file that was kept in a plastic cover fell from his hand and captain Parth picked it up and handed it to him.

'Many many thanks.'

'Most Welcome.'

'Where from?'

'Kanpur.'

'Ok, but here?'

'Name please?'

'Captain Parth.'

'Nice.'

'Sir, May I know your name'

'Of course'

Talking thus, the two of them stepped out of the 'pandaal'.

'How are you here?'

'Sir, my senior Colonel B.K. Singh had sent me here since he was not getting leave.'

'Ok, but the sex celebrity was working against sex slavery, I think he worked for sometime in Iraq also.'

'Sir, I was also with him. America had asked for soldiers from India for fighting in Iraq.'

Parth had reached his car and he shook hands and asked the Professor if he could drop him. The professor replied that he could drop him at the turning ahead. The car stopped after fifteen minutes and Khanna Saheb got down and went his way but the file was left behind in the car. When Captain Parth reached Army Headquarters he saw the file lying in his car. He took the file and went to the rest room.

The attendant came and asked him if he wanted anything, Parth told him to send some coffee.

He sat down in a chair and started reading the headlines of the 'National Herald' and his eye went to the article on the attack carried out by the Islamic State. Five hundred women had been taken prisoners. He went through a gamut of emotions while sipping his coffee and he started thinking about the trending sexual orientations of people. Then he went on to read the file of Professor Khanna. It was the research work done by him.

There was a preface in the book and the biography which was something like this:

Surendra Khanna had written; 'My father was a professor of Anthropology in Punjab. He had told me to do M.A. in Sociology and do research after that.

After doing B.A. from Jawaharlal Nehru College I was doing M.A.D. in Sociology from D.A.V. Degree College. I had obtained 75% in Previous and that is why I got to do my thesis. My Professor was Dr. B.K. Sharma.

The subject of the thesis was 'The daily life of Prostitutes'. I was very enthusiastic about the subject. I had never been to a brothel before. My mentor was more a mentor than a friend. I liked to see movies, play sports and roam around and studies were a drag for me. My father knew him and there was no mobile, laptop or T.V. in those days. Telephone, telegrams and trunk calls were the order of the day. Letter writing was the medium of communication. I had to do my research and had to go abroad where I underwent different experiences. I got the chance to meet different types of people and had to prepare questionnaires before meeting them. This work was not easy and there were many types of problems I faced.

Once the police nabbed me in the red-light area when the sex workers were negotiating a deal. There are certain places in all cities that are ear-marked as red-light areas. In Calcutta there is Sonagachi, Dharamtalla in Bombay, Chowk in Lucknow and Moolganj in Kanpur. The life of these sex workers is hellish. Besides the work, they had to bear with a tainted reputation, oppression and mental torture. They did not earn enough to fulfill their basic needs and they had to do everything to appear good.

There is a network of sex worker that stretches abroad. The Naaz foundation that works for them petitioned the High Court regarding Section 377 of the IPC, that if two adult people are involved in a relationship with mutual consent, it should be outside the purview of article 377. In 2009 the High Court gave the order that relationship between two people of the same sex will not be considered an offence under Article 377 but the Supreme Court had repealed this order but then it reversed its order in a historic judgement.

Many countries have given consent to same sex marriages. Talks regarding the third gender were made and also on their livelihood.

Terrorist organizations had crossed all limits but sometimes government machinery also made a mockery of it. One word cropped up-L.B.G.T.Q. Lesbian women have sex with each other. Similarly when men have same sex relationships they are called gay. B is for bisexual, T is for third gender, and Q is queer. In this manner old traditions were done away with.

Terrorist organizations made the women their sex slaves and behaved cruelly with them and give a bad name to Islam in the name of 'Jihad'.

There was civil war in South Sudan. It came to light in February 2018 that the situation in Pagak city was terrible. The government gave permission to carry out the rape of 1300 women in lieu of a month's salary.

          SACRIFICED LIFE

In some Muslim countries there are some police officials who are fond of using children as objects of sex. Taking advantage of this the terrorist organizations started trading boys between the ages of 16 & 18 in exchange for secret information.

There was one chapter in the context of the sexual pleasure that is derived by our senses from our mental state that was vividly described. My eyes had become heavy as I read it and I decided to take some rest. I got up and lay down on my bed and the thought came to my mind that there were so many people who kept moving towards their destruction and get entangled in their own web.

Captain Parth had to go on a secret mission to Saudi Arabia. Every country has its secret organization whose objective is to gather important information and relay it to the concerned official. Sometimes they lose their lives in these operations. Parth was successful in the mission that he undertook. He was appointed to the team that the Indian government had formed in order to control the network of terror organizations. These organizations have their own guidelines. At some places, terrorist organizations run a parallel government. Their orders have to be followed. If someone refused to obey orders, he was blackmailed or killed. Not only in Iraq, but such organizations were actively working in other countries too. The United Nations was expressing worry but was not able to control these terror organizations.

When Parth read the research paper further his eyes widened in disbelief. Some countries adopt double standards in the context of terrorism. They supported some organizations and opposed others. Surendra Khanna had written in his research papers that his father was a professor of anthropology. He had travelled to Africa and other Muslim countries as well as some developed countries also and also done a psychological analysis of people everywhere. He had written about chemical weapons and also about communist policies and discussed about countries that flouted human rights.

When the talk came to the production and use of chemical weapons the UN expressed concern. It also expressed concern over the use of atomic weapons.

Citing the research work done by his father, Surendra Khanna said that he did not know for which mission he was working but he knew that it was on terrorist organizations that were violating human rights but many governments were also working on this.

Further he gave a description of the first and second world wars. In that there was description of the mental attitude of the defeated countries and concern over the attitude of the victors. After this Surendra Khanna had described some events from his life. Meanwhile Parth got the message that his leave had been cancelled and he should join without any delay.

Terrifying scenes of war

Parth had read about the devastating condition of the people after the first and second world wars. Whatever be the reasons for war, the outcome is terrible. There was a big question looming over humanity. Did we want war or did we want peace? The inhuman acts of the tyrant Adolf Hitler had crossed all limits. It had become second nature with him to send Jews to the gas chambers and kill them by torture. He was a communist and it was the same with Mussolini in Italy. Hitler had given rise to Nazism and Mussolini to fascism. The soldiers obey the State.

When America used atom bombs on Hiroshima and Nagasaki as a last resort, there was outrage in the whole world. Russia was also not happy and even Einstein who was mainly responsible for the technology of the atom bomb was saddened. Hitler committed suicide and Mussolini was publicly by the people. Seeing the ravages of war, man feels a strange restlessness that cannot be described in words.

His plane landed at Baghdad airport. There were about 90 people who deboarded. The team of the army headquarters received him. There were arrangements for him there, and some American officials were also there. There was a secret meeting and the next program was discussed.

Captain Parth vacated a large area that had been under the control of the Islamic State. The sex slaves were released and the situation gradually came under control. America was thinking of recalling its soldiers.

People believe that America has a double standard with regard to terrorist organizations.. Sometimes it made secret pacts with them and the governments of those nations came under its control. There is mutual discord between the countries also; Parth was gradually understanding things.. But it could not make any difference. He had to work for his country and obey the given orders. He had got the network of terrorist organizations under his control. He could hack the network himself.

The terrorists who were with ISIS- Diger-46%, LAtins-42%, LTTE-24%, Jews-7%, Muslims-6%, Communists-5%. 90% of the terrorists in the world are non-Muslims. The real name of Abu Bakr Albada Dadi is Shamoon Elite. The secret agency of France had years ago said that he was an agent who lived in Mosul city of Iraq and lived in a room of a mosque and was taking Islamic education. The commander of Amar Ujala –Siddharth Dhar is an Indian. There is one commander –Prakash- who is sometimes seen. The terrorists give fake names to their secret agents. Saddam Hussian was a tyrant who attacked Kuwait and got it included in Iraq. It is said that there is Shia majority in Kuwait. Citizens of India and Pakistan work there. Saddam Hussain was eventually hanged to death in public and the situation became out of control and America had to send its army.

We will have to ponder over the geographical and historical situation of Iraq.

Iraq is an Islamic country situated in West Asia. It is surrounded by Saudi Arab and Kuwait in the South, Jordan and Syria in the West, Turkey in the north and Iran on the East. A part of Iraq is also surrounded by the Persian Gulf in the South-West. After the fall of Syria, there was western influence in Iraq. After the 6th century there was the influence of Arabs and Islam religion became predominant during this period. Baghdad Abbassi was the capital of the Khilafat. The language spoken is mainly Turkish and Arabic. Religion is 65% Shias and 35% Sunnis. Sadaam Hussain was a Sunni.

Till 1935 Iran was known as Persia. Iran is surrounded by the Caspian Sea in the North, Persian Gulf in the South, Iraq and Turkey in the West and Afghanistan and Pakistan in the East. In 1979 Iran was proclaimed as an Islamic country. Along with the capital Tehran, Isfahan, Tarzeb and Mashad are the major cities. The Iranians had come 2000 years ago from the North and East and they laid the foundation for a mixed culture from which Iran got its identity. The Harwani ruler also used Airam and Aryam. Israel has a parliamentary democracy. It is important to know about it. The state of Israel is situated in the Middle East. In the north it is surrounded by Lebanon, by Syria in the North East, Jordan on the western banks of the East, Egypt and Gaza strip in the South West and the Red sea in the south. This is the only country that is a Jewish majority. It was separated from Philistine on 14th May 1948 and given the status of an independent country. From then till now it has been constantly at war with its neighboring Arab countries and Philistine. The dispute is mainly regarding the Gaza strip, The Western Sinai peninsula and Hiatus. The financial capital is Tel Aviv. This country with a high standard of living is a developed country and is a member of ICD.

There are many reasons for disputes. In such a situation it is difficult to identify between right and wrong. Errors are also of two types-the first ones are natural and the second are conspiratorial.

Parth was considered to be a very able and intelligent officer of the Indian army. He had taken part in many battles.

Obstacles during the research period

He had prepared a long questionnaire for interviewing the prostitutes. But the question was how to approach them? They used to don make-up and sit in the balconies in Moolganj and call their customers by gesture. They had their agents who kept albums of the beautiful girls. He thought he would go in the afternoon. There, I came into contact with an agent and told him my objective; he did not pay much attention to me. It was only when I took him to the canteen and treated him to some snacks that he looked at me. I had no dearth of money, I stayed in the hostel at D.A.V College and there was good arrangement of food.

The person presented an abnormal appearance. He was wearing a 'pyjama kurta' and was of average build but his manner of speaking was very attractive and respectful. He told me that the rates differed, starting from hundred rupees for the youngest and prettiest girl. I gave him 200 rupees that included his commission. He told me that I should let him know if I liked some girl. And he would fix a meeting between us.

I was quite excited and curious and fearful. I wanted to take one companion with me but he was not present at that time. The day and time were fixed. I brought a file and pen and came to the Sindhi hotel where there were mostly Muslims whom I did not like. There was a police chowki in the middle; sometimes goonda-type people also came there and one had to be prepared to deal with them.

He and I entered the lane, some prostitutes started gesturing to me; I thought of the movie 'Pehchan' which had a scene quite like this.

Before that I had seen Guru Dutt's fil 'Pyasa' too. The well known lyricist Sahir Ludhianvi had written its songs. The songs were sung by Mohd Rafi and Hemant Kumar. There were two hit sosn-'Jane ve kaise log the jinko pyar se pyar mila' and the other was 'Kahan Muhafiz khudi jinhe Hind par naaz hai'. I was feeling anxious and I told him that we should do what we had come to do.

I am not feeling ok.

You will have to give money when you come again.

Ok.

We came outside and drank coca-cola. I went to the hostel by a rickshaw after pledging to meet in the hostel the next day. People were talking between themselves. Most of them had jasmine flowers in their hands and some had put fragrance behind their ears. I was astounded to see the type of people who came here but who was I to judge when I had come here myself.

I was looking at the girls standing there. There was a middle- aged lady there with an 18 year- old girl. I gestured to her and he immediately went there and made the deal. The rates for the girl were different. I went with her to the room. The room was not very big but enough to accommodate an 'almirah' and a dressing table. It was seven o' clock in the evening. There was a radio in one corner of the room and a bed in the center on which a beautiful sheet was spread. On it was lying a colorful pillow.

The woman took out a bottle of liquor and two glasses from the almirah and looked at me.

I waved them away. Her daughter was with her awaiting instructions from her mother. She thought that she had had got the entire money and she made me sit down on the bed and told me to remove my clothes.

I told her that she should sit on the bed and I would sit on the chair and talk to her. She took my face in both her hands and started caressing it. A tremor ran through the length of my spine., I wondered what was going on in my body.

'Arre Aunty, stop her from what she is doing'.

Her mother gestured to her to stop but she did not let go of my hands. I told her that I was a student of sociology and was doing research work on them. Hearing this he said, 'Why have you come at this time?' This is our business time.'

I said to her that I had given the money to which she replied that they were for only one hour.

I told her that I would give her more if she wanted me to; this impressed her daughter and she said it was ok. Both of them took a copy of the questionnaire and sat on the bed. I sat on a chair and started questioning them. There was a sudden commotion and we came to know that there had been a police raid. A policeman came and asked me to accompany him to the police station.

The woman wanted to bribe the policeman and be released but he said that his senior was standing below and he would do whatever he was told to do. We started cursing ourselves. I had no one whom I could ring up and ask for help. We reached the police station; I was very restless. The woman assured me that nothing would happen since these people are used to such happenings.

The police officer in-charge was Ram Singh and he was a very honest official. People in the city had a lot of respect for him and the crime rate in Kanpur had come down after his posting here. We were all made to sit on the floor. The police were keeping a lookout everywhere. Ram Singh was carrying out the supervision and his eye fell on me. He shouted at a constable to bring me to his cell. The constable took me to his room and I was asked to sit. I shyly greeted him and he asked me to sit quietly. He asked me why I had gone there and also whether I had come to Banda to study or to ogle at girls. My throat felt parched and was wondering what to say when a soldier cam up and kept two glasses of water and two cups of tea and went away. I gathered my courage and started telling him, 'Where is the document file?' I told him that it was with Pooja and he was surprised that I knew her name too. I told him that I was taking her interview.

The bell rang and the constable came in and he was told to bring Pooja and her mother inside. Both of them came and greeted him respectfully; they were feeling shy to sit down. The police official rang the bell and asked for tea to be brought. Pooja took out the file and gave it to him. Ram Singh started reading it intently. He had been a student of Surendra Khanna's father and had passed the IPS examination under his benevolence. He was in a quandary. In the end, he warned everyone and allowed them tolet them go. He asked Surendra whether he wanted to be dropped to the hostel or whether he wanted to remain there. Surendra replied that he wanted to leave. Surendra was dropped to his hostel. Pooja felt a certain attraction towards Surendra and started thinking of a plan to meet him again.

Parth was reading the research paper when the agent rang up. He wanted to report fast. Those who work for secret missions put their lives in danger. Sometimes they are not able to meet their families for long intervals of time and their entire time is spent in work. They have no other objective except their work. There is always a chance of secrets getting leaked and they always have to keep their brains functioning in top order.

The present technology has become so advanced that man uses it for his advantage but sometimes it proves to be a bane instead of a boon. A race is going on between human and artificial intelligence.

     SACRIFICED LIFE

Artificial intelligence

Parth's brain was no less than a super computer. It was a god -given talent. This was the reason that the Indian government had called him to America when he was giving his services to the army.

Artificial intelligence makes the machines so intelligent that they can dwell on intelligent thinking. It happens in the same manner that humans use their intelligence to go about their daily lives, learn, think and then make decisions.

Two nations are working in the haste of e-way. China is constantly making newer machines in its laboratories because it wants to become the biggest power in the world. But where there are gains, there is danger also.

The United Nations has given guidelines for the welfare of the world. It has made laws under the 'Protection of Human Rights Act, 1993'.

It came to light that Russia had used the atom bomb against Iran, but it has not accepted this.

In the second world war there was a huge loss of life due to the use of atom bombs because of the radio active substances released in the atmosphere that are still affecting people in Germany.

Many writers wrote imaginary novels in which they depicted the mental suffering of the people that came true in the future. 'The Eyes of Darkness' was written by Dem Koontz in 1981.On page 553, it was written that the corona virus was made in a laboratory in Wuhan in China in a secret manner. China wanted to use it in the form of a biological weapon. China brought it in use in 2020 but it proved deadly for china itself.

The entire world is paying for this act of China's. Millions of people have lost their lives. Lakhs are infected and the situation is terrifying. America has clamed the WHO for siding with China. Now the question is whether the virus is man-made or natural.

The corona virus brought the world to a standstill. All countries imposed a lockdown. Is there any limit to meanness? There is no antidote for corona virus; the only protection is vaccination. Corona can be defeated with awareness and alertness. Countries even had to call out the army in defense against it. This pandemic is no less than a world war.

In India an all India curfew was imposed on the country on 22nd March 2020 that was successful. The country showed its gratefulness to all those who gave their services in fighting the virus by the blowing of conches and by thumping 'thalis'.

The virus stood as a challenge for the entire country. The economic condition of the entire country took a beating. Industries and businesses came to a standstill.

Crises are of two types- the first ones are natural and the second are those that are man-made. Both cause loss to human beings.

The form of loyalty

The biggest cyber crime to take place in the world was on 28th November 2013. The police of five countries investigated it. The attackers used the technique of 'Distributed Denial of Service', in which the subject is sent a lot of traffic so that he becomes out of range. Internet services get disrupted because of this.

When AI is developed there is an increase of human-beneficial services but chances of misuse increase. People with a criminal bent of mind use it for their own selfish ends and destroy the system. Parth needs such officials to bring such situations under control. This cyber war cannot be won by physical force, but by artificial intelligence.

It becomes necessary to meditate on the nature and lives of scientists, doctors, traders, politicians, security personnel, administrators, etc. Every nation has its own benefits to secure and it does so by remaining under a distinct boundary. Some rule the people through democratic means, some as kings and some by belief in the Islamic system. There is a system of considering the king to be one's representative. With time adages such as 'Kings never do wrong' become 'Change is the law of Nature.'

In the Mahabharata there is one scene between Bhisma and Vidur. Bhisma was loyal towards the King's throne whereas Vidur was a believer of loyalty. The difference was that Bhishma was compelled to support the wrong policies of the king because of his loyalty towards the throne. Externally he had to show his support, even though he may be revolting internally. Opposite to this, Vidur had no such compulsions and he used to oppose such policies. There was a very slight difference between the loyalties of the two. Even today there are such people. Divine powers make their appearance from time to time and are the needs of times. At one time the study of the Vedas was taboo due to certain reasons. Sanskrit in an invaluable resource.

66 This text can be read by anyone.

According to ancient Hindu religion, i.e, according to Sanatan theory the final objective of human life is to gain 'moksha' or salvation. Three paths lead to it and these are 'Gyan Maarg', 'Karmyog' and 'Bhakti Maarg'. All three complement each other; by treading these three paths a person can be come free of rebirths. The synopsis of this can be found in the Mahabharta. ShriKrishna has said about it from his own –its description is not available anywhere.

Aadi Parv-

Antaryami Narayan Swaroop Bhagwaan Shri Krishna-

The Bhsihma Parv of ShrimadBhagvadgeeta includes the Mahabharata. This is known as the best psychological book of Geeta.

There come such moments in every person's life where he has to face war like situations. Even after the passing away of so many eras there characters are alive today. What sort of formation did Bhsihma make with his small army?

Sanjay was telling Dhritrashtra the situation of war. Dritrashtra was wishing for his son's victory. He was thinking that it would be difficult for Bhsima to penetrate the chakrvyuh (circular array of military troops).

Here Yudhishthir was worried. Arjun believed that the chakrvyuh was impenetrable.

The one support left was Shri Krishna, one has to center all of one's energy at one spot. When the energy is focused victory becomes certain- this is a universal principle. KrishnaGovind asked Parth-'Sakha, tell me what I should do? I feel incapable of breaking the chakrvyuh'.

On Parth's becoming sad he said, 'You should remember Durga'. He started describing the greatness of Mahima. Accordingly, Parth started paying attention to Durga- 'You are the one famous by the names of Maha Kali and Kumari Kali, my respects to you. You are Tarini because you curse the sinners. The description of your physical body is very difficult, I bow to you. You are Katyanini and you are the one who assumes a demonic form. You are the one who is famous by the name of Vijaya and Jaya.. Your forehead is adorned with a peacock feather, and different types of ornaments adorn your body. You were born in the family of Nandgop and therefore you are the younger sister of ShriKrishna and have the best qualities and talents. You were very happy by killing Mahishasur. You are also famous as Kaushiki because of being born in the Kushik gotra. When you laugh loudly on looking at enemies, your face becomes as bright as the sun. You are full of compassion-there is no beginning or end to you. You are the ultimate truth and eternal. War is very dear to you. I bow to you a thousand times. The goddess who has assumed the names of Shakambri, Shweta, Hiranyani, Virupakshi and Sudhumrakshi, a thousand bows to you. You are very pure and divine. You have the strength of fire and Jammu Katra is your regular abode. You are well versed in all fields of knowledge. You are the mother of Kartikeya and reside in inaccessible places. Swadha, Swaaha, Kala Saraswati, Vedmata Savitri and Vedanta- are all your names'.

Mahadevi! I have praised you with a clean conscience, may your blessings be with me in this battle of life. Mother, you reside in inaccessible places and even in hell. You defeat demons in war. You are the one who enhances he brilliance of the sun and the moon. You are the priceless jewel of the rich people.

The goddess appeared in the sky and divine light entered the eyes and heart of Parth.

Parth wondered where he was he had seen all of this in his dreams. He started thinking that this was some superhuman power and we were not capable of understanding it. Whatever is manifested externally is but a form of the internal power! Determination is nothing but the ability to adapt to adverse circumstances.

When Hitler was trying to become the most powerful person in this world, he had caused devastation. For outward purposed, he had committed suicide but it was the energy of the great person Arvind Ghosh that had compelled him to commit suicide. We need some definite sources to understand mental strength.

Parth had been given different types of trainings that he had learnt and could even practice. There were challenges at the global level and India was in trouble. He was put under the care of a guru.

Conspiracy

From times immemorial people and the governments, terrorist organizations and extremists work for their own good. They have their own constitutions and their objectives. They hatch conspiracies for their ulterior objectives. Some intelligent people are required to unveil their insidious designs. The one who has a superior brain is able to establish himself.

During the time of the Mahabharata the Kauravas tried to play dirty with the Pandavas many times. The evil idea of constructing the wax house and burning the Pandavas to death was that of was foiled because of

Vidur. One can find many other examples like this. Ravana hatched many conspiracies to bring about the downfall of Ram. And in the end he himself died. Eras change and characters change but human nature remains much he same. Today also there are 'Rams' and 'Ravans's amongst us.

In most of the countries secret information is purchased and sold. Politicians and reporters are part of this nexus.

The defense department experiments through the medium of the army under it and purchases and sells arms. The role of the main administrators of the nation and the army is very important in this. Most people want to live a life of luxury and comfort, but against this there are some who are honest and fulfill their responsibilities with all sincerity.

It is true that everything is human made but there are some natural phenomena that protect those are loyal. The relationships between good people and bad people go on and sometimes they are sweet and sometimes bitter.

Even though there was dissent within the family. Parth joined the army because he respected Bhishma Narayan Sharma's feelings.

There is a procedure for joining the defense department. The competitors have to give a test and are given training if they are successful. Whenever there is a situation of war in the country, people are inducted. During emergencies, those who are physically eligible and have a good intelligence are chosen after tough examination. Those who are especially capable are inducted into the defense department. Along with physical capability, mental intelligence is also taken into account.

Parth underwent training from the Military Academy in Dehradun. He met many people during the training. There his life revolved around his colleagues, training, guest- lectures ad pledges taken to die in service of the country.

After the training was over it was announced that they would be commissioned for which a party was thrown. There are some junior commissioned officers during the training who are very strict ; they make you work very hard and make you as tough as iron. Some higher officials hold meetings with the trainees and take information about the cadets. They talk about their capabilities and their quick decision-making abilities because they are the ones who will lead the nation during a war.

One such strict officer was Colonel Naseem. Abiding by the rules and regulations and making others do so was an important part of his life. He got quite attached to Parth during the training. He recommended his name for special training in which they are made to undergo very difficult training. Shivers run down peoples' spines when they think of this training. It was in Lieutenant Parth's nature to break rules and he was a jovial person.

With the passage of time Lieutenant Parth got promoted and became a captain and he joined the Ordinance factory under Colonel Naseem.

France was about to sign a treaty with India over the purchase of arms; a panel was formed for this. Many officers of the rank of Brigadier were part of this and Lieutenant Naseem was in it. Naseem was an honest and daring officer.

Lieutenant Naseem inspected the arms very carefully and they did not pass the standards. He refused to give permission for their purchase, whereas the others had given their consent for the purchase. The deal was for 1.2 billion rupees. All the people in the panel had their commissions in the deal, except for the Colonel.

There is a lot of carelessness in the defense department. The people there are deep in corruption and make a mockery of the country but sometimes there are some intelligent and honest defense ministers and realize the problems faced by the soldiers and take adequate steps. The temperatures in Siachen fall to sub-zero levels. The soldiers need clothing according to these temperatures. They used to send indented letters of requirement-either the material was not supplied or it was done in inadequate amounts or of inferior quality and there was no one to address their grievances.

When George Fernandez was the defense minister and toured the Siachen area he came to know that the soldiers did not have appropriate materials. He told his secretary to stay there for 15 days and see for himself how the soldiers lived in such adverse circumstances and still worked for the country. He was recalled after 3 days.

The country faces more danger from people in the country who pose as friends rather than from our enemies from outside the country; we have to fight both and we need brave soldiers for that.

When china invaded India in 1962, India's Prime Minister was Jawaharlal Nehru. Looking at the time and the situation he adopted the policy of non-alignment but it proved counter-productive later on.

In September 1946 after the establishment of the interim government the Indian foreign policy was developed. Pandit Nehru made it clear that India would support a free policy and would not be a party to any faction.

 SACRIFICED LIFE

India would oppose colonialism and caste differences in any part of the world and would assist those countries that were for world peace. The policy of non-alignment proved dangerous for India and it was greatly criticized.

During the time of China's aggression in 1962, the policy of non-alignment was in for a trial by fire. Many critics made bitter criticisms of India's non- alignment and there was talk of doing away with this policy. India supported the freedom of Africa's newly independent states, but when China invaded India there was no support from anywhere. Although western nations like America, England, Canada, West Germany immediately sent war arsenals to India via air.

After China's aggression in 1962, the then ambassador of America, Galbraith, said on 6th November 1962 that America would send arms to India within 90 hours. Initially the Soviet Union refused to help India, but seeing America's influence it also sent its MIG planes and also promised to build a factory for manufacturing these planes. Nehru was enamored of his own foreign policy and because of his desire for international fame he caused a huge loss to the country although he did get some success in resolving some foreign matters.

The differences between America and North and South Korea were a matter of concern for the policy makers in America. There were four world super-powers involved in it. Japan had decided to side with South Korea and the Soviet Union was on North Korea's side.

Nations have to watch out for their own interests. America was badly entangled in the Vietnam War. It had suffered great losses in the war. After using its discretion and talking with China, it set Vietnam free.

At that time Parth was deliberating on the 2nd world war. A defense official has to have knowledge of the wars that have taken place in history. Groups are formed on the basis of self-interest. Regarding arms deals, many times it has been seen that even the heads of government have allegations leveled against them. When governments change the defense policies also change. In the Bofors matter the then Prime Minister was the culprit and the ex Prime Minister Vishwnath Prasad Singh had opposed the deal. One does not know the truth of the matter but Rajeev Gandhi was given a clean chit in the matter.

It came to light that many famous and rich personalities have their accounts in Swiss banks and many eminent leaders of India including Rajeev Gandhi were present in that list. It is an undisputed fact that there is a lot of unconstitutional give and take in defense deals

Parth was posted under commanding officer Lieutenant Colonel Naseem Ahmed in Delhi Military Headquarter. A deal was being struck with a French company to supply arms. Brigadier A.K. Singh was himself taking an interest in the deal. Since the material was not up to the standards, Colonel Naseem gave an adverse report on it. He was put under pressure by Brigadier Singh, but he did not relent from his position and a conspiracy was hatched to get him involved in a bribery matter. After this there was no obstacle in the deal being made.

Captain Parth was working in his laboratory. An encrypted message arrived by mistake on Parth's code but was immediately deleted. Parth was in shock. IF he gave that message to Colonel Naseem Brigadier Singh would be finished; if he did not give the message to Colonel Naseem the CBI would arrest colonel Naseem. He was in a dilemma. Colonel Naseem's daughter- Fatima- had come home in the holidays. They had worked together on a mission. She had been kept in a cell that was associated with Parth too. Parth's brain reeled-he thought he could not go to the Colonel's house without reason after neglecting his duty.

At the instigation of the Brigadier, Colonel Naseem's house was raided at 7 o'clock in the evening. IT was a winter night and the entire house was surrounded. A search warrant was produced and the house was searched. Colonel Naseem was at a loss to understand what was going on. A CBI officer told him that he had been alleged to have taken a bribe of 3 lakh rupees in a defense deal. The colonel told them to search the house with pleasure. Nothing was found in an operation that lasted for four hours. All the officers were surprised. Nobody had paid any attention to Lieutenant Fatima; she had left for a hospital half an hour back for a medical check-up. Colonel Naseem was saved but many questions remained; his honesty came under doubt.

A meeting took place between the CBI officers and the Brigadier. It continued for a long time. At the end a secret decision was taken what the Colonel should be murdered at the time of ...when nobody would have any suspicion. Colonel Naseem was going to take part in the ... when Parth gave him the order of the Lieutenant General and this foiled the attempt of the enemies. Each activity of the Colonel was closely monitored.

When Captain Parth gave the news to Fatima in code language she was in shock; she immediately became active. Avoiding the camera she took out the packet containing three lakh rupees from a drawer and came for the medical check-up. She also came to know that her cook Hussain was giving all information to the Brigadier. The Brigadier had links with a terrorist organization.

The opposition was worried after this incident and others. Lieutenant Fatima told the Colonel about Captain Parth and said that the danger was not yet over and everything should be kept secret.

The deal with the French company was not concluded but was stalled for sometime. The company had already spent quite a large amount of money for the deal. She wanted the deal to take place soon and the supply should resume. Brigadier Singh started disliking Captain Parth because he suspected that he was shielding Colonel Naseem. Keeping this in mind eh recommended Captain PArth's name for the squad going to Iraq, but meanwhile Parth was assigned for special duty to the cyber branch cell and it proved terrible for the Brigadier.

Colonel Naseem was transferred to the anti terror group on the Kashmir border. The colonel had been saved but a departmental enquiry was instigated against him for not giving a right report in the purchase of the aircraft. The planes that had been purchased had some internal defects as regards their structure because of which several planes had crashed. The crashes were not properly investigated after the black boxes were found. The allegation on Colonel Naseem was that despite being a mechanical engineer he had not paid attention to the design of the plane's engine.

Many times it has been seen that there is a difference of opinion between the head of a country and the army chief. There have been many army chiefs who have refused to obey the instructions of the head of the nation. The army chiefs are aware of their subjects while the heads of nations have a general idea of such things. Sometimes there is rebellion and the army chief takes the power in his hands and announces himself to be the head of state and there are many examples of the political leaders being overthrown and a military ruler taking over the reins of the country.

Sometimes it becomes imperative to have military rule during times of anarchy and therefore it is necessary to have a democratic system to prevent inhuman behavior.

Invisible strength and energy

The demented mentality of Osama Bin Laden -the head of the terror organization led to the killing of over 3000 people in the terror attack of 9th September 2001. The brave soldiers of America killed him by entering into Pakistan. The first question about this attack was-what led him to carry out such a heinous attack-the second –one Jew was also present in the tower at the time and the third why was such an advanced country like America unaware of the impending attack? There must surely have been some laxity in the alertness.

Parth was thinking along these lines –he had taken a special training from a meditator sitting in the lap of the Himalayas. He envisioned another route to reach there.

A train was stopped at a small station and a mahatma got down to buy some things, but could not get anything. He was speaking in English and nobody could understand him. Then he went to the Station Master's room where a young man was sitting. The Station Master was respectful with the Mahatma who asked him if he could get something to eat.

He ordered a person to get something to eat and very soon some eatables arrived, like samosas and tea. The mahatma gave a banana to the young man. All three of them wanted the other person to eat first. All of them had tea. Before eating anything the Mahatma looked towards the sky and uttered some words. After that he would eat.

The Mahatma took out a ten- rupee note from his pocket and wanted to give it to the Station Master. The Station Master refused saying that he was a retired major and was doing some research work and that is why he was going to a great seer. He gave the money for the tea and eatables for all of them.

There was some talk on geographic administration and the Station Master said he could give some tips if the young man wanted to enter the defense services. But the man said he had no such intention. Even then he told him of a place in Uttarakhand where he could go and meditate and he would get the 'darshan' of Onkar Swami. He was a 'trikalagya' He told the man that because of the intense sacrifices of his ancestors he had been bestowed with special qualities and that he would enter the defense forces. He would set the innocent officers free. He was given a special mantra and was explained how to say the mantra and also explained some natural principles of nature. When the mahatma touched the young man's body it seemed to him that a current had passed through it.

Meanwhile the whistle of the train blew. The major entered his compartment and the young man was none other than Captain Parth.

When he saved Colonel Naseem from the conspirators he started recalling the previous incidents. He had passed many trainings. According to him the writer of a true story has a main character and the writer gives

  SACRIFICED LIFE

him a character by his words. After reading the book the readers try to adapt themselves according to the character. Although there is no place in the vedas for the doctrine of reincarnation, Ved Vyas has used this in the Dwapar era in the Mahabharata. In this manner the writer imagines an actor and who emerges as a hero or a villain in the minds of people and influences them in a positive or negative manner.

Great people like Vishnu, Brahma, Shankar, Ram, Parshuram, Krishna, Mahatama, Gautam Budha, Paigambar Hazrat Muhammad and Jesus Christ were all people who were full of positivity and came to this earth for the welfare of the world. They inspire people to do good and spread lightness of the 'One God'.

Parth had undertaken many types of trainings. He had learnt how to operate land vehicles, air vehicles and water vehicles. He also had commando training which is very difficult and also learnt the art of less military might prevailing over a stronger military might. He had also learnt the art of espionage.

The secret tests of America started getting leaked which was a cause of concern. A few months before this, Parth had given his resignation from the American company and left for India. The company had the entire record of his capability. Assange had been a military officer in America and working in the field of journalism. He was the director of Wilkinson New channel. He had received the secret news of most of the major countries. He also had the reports of who had accounts in Swiss banks.

The scientists and experts of America and other countries were thinking that they were helpless. The government of India requested government of America for the services of Parth for one month. The Indian government realized the value of his services.

The defense ministry of India talked to the General. He had sent Parth to Iraq for three months under a treaty made with America. IT was a secret mission. The situation in Iraq was very bad. The Islamic State had included some other organizations in its fold and was spreading terror.

Cyber crime was not coming under control and many banks had collapsed. This was the situation in Iraq also but Parth had destroyed the entire network of the terror organizations. They had lost their nerve.

How Parth had managed to get hold of a secret report was a mystery. There was a video clip in which about two hundred women were being forcibly taken abroad on a ship. Osama Bin Laden had taken them prisoners through his organization-most of the women belonged to the

Shia community. This incident was being connected to the 9/11 terror attacks but all this was imaginary.

National Security

Questions come to be raised on the style of functioning of the defense officials if the entire responsibility of the country's security depends on the head of the country and the army chief and they have difference of opinion on it.

The role of America in the Bangladesh crisis of 1971 and the India-Pakistan war remain strange. On 25th March 1971, Pakistan launched an offensive on the beleaguered people of East Pakistan on the orders of the Pakistani government of Yahya Khan. Because of this the onus of feeding and giving asylum to about one crore victims of East Pakistan fell on India. India made a complaint to America that Pakistan was misusing America's arms and urged America that since Pakistan came under its sphere of influence, Nixon's government should put pressure on Pakistan to stop atrocities in East Pakistan and stop the refuges from entering India. America shrugged it off saying that it was India and Pakistan's internal affair. Pakistan kept getting military and other aid. Smt. Indira Gandhi went to America on 6th November 1974 in order to explain India's stance, but Nixon did not accept this logic. America received a great setback after India and Russia signed the friendship treaty in August 1971.

A war broke out between India and Pakistan on 3rd December 1971. Before the war began Indira Gandhi held a secret meeting with the government of India and the then Field Marshal of the army, Sam Maneckshaw was present in it. He was ordered to attack Pakistan but he refused to obey the orders. Smt Indira Gandhi was angered beyond limits and said that he couldn't disobey the orders. Maneckshaw replied that for one thing it was the rainy season and the rivers and canals were overflowing and he needed two months for preparation.

Indira Gandhi admitted that sometimes such situations arise when differences crop up between the Army Chief and the head of the country.

There are many countries where there has been a civil war. There was a coup in Pakistan in 1971 when General Zia-ul-Haq snatched the power from the hands of the Prime Minister, Zulfiquar Ali Bhutto and got him hanged in the Rawalpindi Central jail. His daughter Benazir Bhutto was also a assassinated. Similarly Pervez Musharraf got power by using his military might. Such incidents frequently take place in Islamic countries. The Indian Constitution is the world's best Constitution. Army officials

    SACRIFICED LIFE

should have such knowledge and also knowledge about the current history and politics of the world.

After Saddam Hussain was given the death sentence in Iraq the situation there was very bad. A civil war had erupted. While the American forces were standing by the terror organizations were carrying out their activities. Parth was thinking that most of the terror organizations had their head quarters in America and it was always using double standards.

IT is true that in the 1962 war between India and China, the Western countries like America and Britain supported India openly.

On 18th May 2018, Gina Hospell was made the chief of the supreme investigating agency of America, the CIA. Hospell has been connected to the CIA for more than 30 years, and for the first time a woman has been appointed to this prestigious post.

She is the first woman director in more than 70 years. She was born on 1st October 1956 in Ashland County. After the 9/11 attack the opposition had criticized her for her role in the CIA enquiry.

After the error made by the CIA many officers were regarded with suspicion but with the support of 66 democratic senators they were victorious in the voting where they got 54 and the opposition got 45 votes. On 14th May 2018 America opened its embassy in the Jewish city of Jerusalem which upset the Arab nations. The culprit in the Purulia arms dropping case KimDavies could not be brought to India by saying that it was a case of human rights violation.

Military formation

As soon as he came back from Iraq, Parth was court martialled. Brigadier Singh felt that as long as Captain Parth was there, his life was in danger. There were very serious charges leveled against him. The terror organization was from Kurd although it did not come under that category.

United Air Lines Flight 175 hits the south tower of the World Trade Center during the September attacks of 2001 in New York City. Terrorism in the broadest sense is the use of international violence generally against civil lives for political purposes. It is used to primarily refer to violence during peace time or context of war against non combatants (mostly civil lives & neutral military persons) The Terms 'Terrorist & Terrorism" originated during the French revolution of the late 18th century but gained mainstream popularity in 1970 in news reports and books covering the conflicts in Northern Ireland and the Basque Country and Palestine. The increased use of suicide attacks was typified by the September 11 attacks in New York city and Washington D.C. in 2001.

Government and non-state groups use the term to abuse or denounce opposing groups. Various political groups have been accused of using terrorism to achieve the objectives. The organization, nationalist groups, religious groups, revolutionary groups and government legislation declaring terrorism a crime has been adopted in many states. When terrorism is perpetrated by nation states it is not considered terrorism by the state perpetrating it. There is no consensus whether or not terrorism should be regarded as a war crime. The Global Terrorism Database maintained by the University of Moreland College has recorded 61000 incidents of new-state terrorism resulting in at least 14000 deaths between 2000 and 2014.

Vanshika, secret agent of India was doing research on the emotional state of the terrorist organizations and the manner in which the countries dealing with terrorism. Captain Parth was also a part of this mission. The U.S. was adopting double standards; the incidents that were taking place in Iraq were extremely horrendous. America violated the Geneva pact many times. There were some important points that showed the negative view point of America. These were:

1. America looked at the rest of the world with a biased feeling to fulfill its own selfish interests.
2. It was behaving like a big daddy and supplying arms to Arab countries.
3. It wanted to keep a control over the oil producing countries.
4. It gives a wrong inventory.
5. At some places it opposes India's non-aligned policy, at other times it keeps quiet.
6. Cold war between the U.S. and Soviet Union.
7. Makes use of the dual policy in matters of disarmament.
8. America openly opposed the Geneva pact during the war.
9. The terrorists treated the captives very cruelly but America was no less and the women commanders crossed all limits by making the war soldiers march naked.
10. Its policies not only influenced the Arab countries but also other countries.
11. The law and order in many countries was very proper but the mentality of the people was not right.

12. America is the headquarters of most of the terrorists.

13. The main points of the Geneva pact were that bombarding would not be done on religious places, places of refuge and hospitals.

The war captives would be treated in accordance with the rules.

After the fall of Syria, foreign powers have held sway in Iraq. The capital of Iraq is Baghdad, the language is Arab, the population is 3,123,4000, the area is 438317 square kms and there are 65% Shias and 35% Sunnis.

The war prisoners were kept in terrorist camps. The women were kept as sexual slaves. The terrorists captured a place 80 kms. from Baghdad and the army was helpless to do anything. If bombarding was carried out there was the danger of innocent people getting killed.

Captain Parth was given the command under a special plan but was kept deprived of arms and other requirements, but nanotechnology was secretly used. The commander-in-chief did not know of this. The terrorists got to know of the activities going on there. Parth prepared the strategy for the operation.

Parth recalled the 'Internet of Things' known as IOT in short. One should not attack till the whereabouts of the enemy are properly known. Technology expert, Win Ashton of Britain has done work on this subject. Parth made a plan of keeping small capsule sized detonators in a small box and obtaining the release of the war prisoners by attacking at 11 o'clock. There were 7 people in the team. One Indian army team was doing some other work. Terrorists were keeping a lookout in the camp and the soldiers had reached quite near the camp. Some soldiers were forcibly taking a woman and it was clear that they were going to sexually exploit her. One could not see her face clearly but it was clear that she was fair and well-built and was trying to get free. PArth killed one of the soldiers on guard in one stroke and wearing his uniform he reached the camp. Parth gestured using sign language and got the woman released and shot two soldiers with his silence revolver. The woman was well trained and it did not take her long to give information regarding the captives and the camps. All the terrorists were killed in the surprise attack and the women prisoners were sent by truck to Baghdad. Parth told the terrorists that the women prisoners should be handed over to him and if that was not done, he would take the foreign reports as hostages. Parth was trying to give information to Vanshika but it was not reaching her. The Indian army was sent but they did not have the road map and it was a question of rescuing the people.

The vehicles were moving towards Baghdad with the war prisoners on board. He dialled a number. One ISIS group came under my control 80 kms north of Baghdad. Captain Parth speaking 091-this was the message that was the reason was his court martial. The army unit and everyone else was rescued and 50 people of the ISIS were killed. This incident was removed from the records and the situation in Iraq had improved a lot.

Parth had done everything for human good and he should be lauded, whereas the people sitting in India had given a proposal for his court martial.

By the time the Indian army came back from Iraq, Parth's health had deteriorated. He went on medical leave and his health was constantly deteriorating. Parth sent a brief history of himself to Vanshika. He was conducting a secret investigation of an IPS officer, Ramesh Shriavstava of Kolkatta. He had to give the report in three days and she wanted to talk to Parth with regard to this. S.S. Shrivastava had sold secret photographs to a foreign company and among them were some photographs that were directly related to the defense services.

Mental peace

Parth could recall a very old incident when a retired major who had taken 'sanysas' had told him that he would meet Om Swami and he would reveal many of nature's secrets to him.

Our country is rich in people who are well- versed in various fields of life. Om Swami resided in an ashram in Uttarakhand in the foothills of the Himalayas. He used to meditate in peace and Parth's meeting with him was indeed a coincidence.

The truth is that the inner conscience of each human being is worth of love because it is the essence of our being. The creative force of the Universe is present in each one of us. The divine element that creates and consumes this earth manifests itself as our soul.

Some schools of thought do not accept the presence of a soul. Gautam Buddha also did not accept the presence of a God and soul although he preaches the attainment of supreme consciousness through meditation and non-violence. The Buddhist religion has given us a lot of systems. Most of the kings accepted his sayings and adopted Buddhism. The great emperor Ashoka also believed in Buddhism.

The Vedic Sanatan religion accepted Gautam Buddha in the form of Vishnu. It is worth mentioning that in the Vedas there is no place for God as a form. It was Ved Vyas who propounded the theory of reincarnation and in the Geeta, Shri Krishna who was endowed with all the good qualities has given instructions to the great marksman, Parth.

In the 'Geeta', two ways have been described by for the attainment of enlightenment- one is 'Sankhya Yog' and the second is 'Karmyog'.

Every substance is like a mirage and not having the feeling that you are responsible for being the doer of any work and being at one with the Supreme Lord is 'Sankhya Yog' and 'Karmyog' is the belief that everything belongs to God and keeping a balance and being free of the desire for getting the fruits of one's action and being respectful in mind and speech and dedicating oneself mentally and physically at God's feet and constantly meditating on God's name and his qualities.

Working at the mental level is a natural process for mankind and research is done on this as the person works on his inner form, the more his energy gets manifested. This is the supreme truth. I am really nobody, I am only a channel even that Divine Almighty.

Recalling the words of the 'sanyasi', Parth reached Badrinath, Uttarakhand. According to the beliefs in Hindu tradition, many popular rites are conducted by the best 'pujaris' and 'purohits' in order to provide peace to the departed souls of the devotees who flock there. The ashram was constructed within the perimeter of about one kilometer. And it had four gates. One was for all devotees and visitors and three other gates were for people who wanted to perform special prayers. Along with the ashram there was a temple dedicated to Shiva and Shankar and another temple that did not contain any idol. IT was specially constructed. Inside the sanctorum there was a four-tiered ground, on top of which was a layer of sacrificial grass on which there was a silken cloth that was filled with a foam like substance. There were about hundred such seats and were kept at a distance of about one meter from each other. In front there was a dais and on a one square feet of black cloth, the word Om was written in shining white color. This was the cell of the devotees.

Parth was unwell but because of his will power he entered the ashram of Omkar Swami.

The door was beautifully etched in wood and the forms of different Gods and Goddesses was engraved on it. In between there was a marble laid path. On both sides were trees and a row of shrubs that were a foot high. Behind one could see a garden laid out with soft green grass. The boundary of the lawn was adorned with different types of flowers that were a delight to the eyes.

Omkar Swami bore a striking resemblance to God Shiva's form. He was six foot tall and healthy looking with big eyes and an attractive face-beholding him gave the devotees a certain happiness. His body was giving out the odor of a light fragrance that smelt like a mixture of sandalwood and rose and was creating a unique ambience.

There was a gymnasium in the ashram where there were different types of exercising equipment. There were also residences for students and trainers and it could be called a university. The students were trained in all things.

Parth introduced himself to the guard sitting at the entrance door. On seeing his attractive personality the doorman thought that he must be possessing some special talent; he immediately let him enter and requested him to sit down and ordered the helper to get water for him. A glass of lukewarm water was brought in a glass and given to Captain Parth; taking the glass he thanked the bearer. Hearing the bearer's reply he realized that the people here were very cultured and he sent his message to the Swami. After some time he was taken to a well decorated room and was told to take a eat and food would be shortly sent for him. Parth asked him if he could have some tea or coffee and he was assured that it would be sent soon.

Parth was feeling happy to be amidst such a beautiful environment and thinking that the saint was surely a learned one. His mind wandered to calamities that were both man-made and natural and the problems they brought with them. The religious texts describe them in great detail. His wandering thoughts were interrupted by the arrival of his lunch. After having his lunch he lay down on the bed and slept.

Each person has a dual consciousness-one that is aware and the second is the sub-conscious mind. Consciousness is that state of mind when we do things in a state of wakefulness. And unconscious mind is the state of sleep and what we think and do during our sleep. Compared to our conscious mind the strength of our unconscious mind is much more and that is why what we can imagine and do in our unconscious mind is not possible in the wakeful state, like going into our pre-birth state or seeing our future.

In reality if we concentrate our waking and non-waking mind in the same direction we can achieve a lot of success.

Knowledge is a bottomless sea and if we manage to obtain even a few drops of this knowledge, man can do wonders. The progress that we see today is a result of a concentration of human mind.

SACRIFICED LIFE

Omkar Swami's cell had been made by keeping in mind the science of Vast. The door of the room was in the East and also had two windows with large transparent panes. The flooring was done in marble. There was a big round table and five revolving chairs were placed around it. Behind the head of the table there was a large framed picture with the word 'Om' written on it. The word was written in a square box from which rays were seen emanating. On the wall opposite this was the picture of a smaller 'Om' that was hung two feet from the roof.

It was four o'clock in the evening. A cool wind was blowing and clouds were moving around in the sky. The warmth of the sun's rays was getting dimmer and the weather was extremely pleasant.

The bearer was taking Parth to meet Omkar Swami. They were talking to each other but on no particular topic; Parth was feeling a kind of happiness in the gentle environs of the ashram.

Meeting people and being separated from them, the occurrence of incidents, the turning of nights into days, eras passing away- all these are pre-determined by God. These are very deep enigmas that are difficult to fathom and if we are able to unravel even an atom of this enigma our life becomes blessed. When a person enters a state of 'alfa' he is aware of his existence and he feels as if he has entered into a state of bliss, but the state does not last long.

If some thought crosses his mind in this state, then according to the all pervasive theory he should attain whatever he desires-there is no doubt in this.

Om Swami was sitting in his revolving chair in his room. In his hands he held a book named, 'Spiritual philosophy and the use of power' that he was reading. There was enough light in the room. Parth entered with the assistant behind him. Before entering the assistant humbly took permission to enter. Parth greeted him with folded hands and said that he had come to seek guidance. Om Swami raised his hands in blessing and said," Do the work that you have been assigned and dedicate your life towards your country and indicated with his hand that Parth should sit down. He had a slight smile on his face an asked after Parth's wellbeing and said that he had to do a lot of good work. Parth told him that he was going through mental and physical illness to which the swami replied that very great soldier had to face such circumstances in life.

Parth asked him the solution to his problems and was told that he was invited just for that. Parth replied that he was an inferior being and even though he was an army officer, but because of the terrible circumstances and the conspiracies being hatched against the country, he felt bewildered and his strategy, intelligence and skill was being unsuccessful against the enemy and his body was losing the battle. He wanted to be protected by the all Supreme. His eyes became awash with tears. It seemed as if Shri Krishna had imbibed all the qualities and had appeared before him in the form of Omkar Swami.

Omkar Swami blessed him to be at mental peace and explained to him the principles of Yoga and trained him. Parth recovered fully and became adept at Rajyog.

Parth became extremely humble. He very humbly requested- Honorable God like being, now I want to take Samadhi.

Omkar Swami told him that the time for it had not yet arrived and he had to do a lot of work for the country. Parth wanted to know why he was being denied the heavenly pleasure.

PAramhans RamKrishna had given the teaching of 'Karmyog' to swami Vivekanand and he brought honor to India by his deeds and expounded the principles of Indian spiritualism.

Swami Vivekanand's name is counted among the greatest sages of the world. I thank you on behalf of the different communities of Hindus.

I am proud to be the follower of such a religion that has provided credibility to different religions of the world. Not only do we believe in compassion, but consider all religions to be true and try to imbibe their teachings. I am proud to be the citizen of such a country that has given its support to all the victimized and boycotted castes on this earth.

Communalism, narrow-mindedness and the religious bigotry arising out of this have ruled over this earth for a very long time. The world has collapsed under the weight of heinous oppression, civilizations have been laid waste because of the atrocities carried out by hate mongering people. If all this had not been the human race would have been much more developed by now. I hope that the bells that were rung in honor of this conference today will be the death-knell for all the fascists and for the mutual bitterness that is there between the people today.

Swami Vivekanand speech was a reverberation of his guru's preachings. 'PArth you have to do carry out a religious war for your nation. I will rid you of all your mental and physical problems and make you a great warrior and provide you a secret knowledge with which you will be able to transmit your messages to anyone without any mechanism. Not only this, you will be able to recognize the entire mental make-up of a person by looking at his forehead.

Omkar Swami gave the special training to Parth and he became a great warrior. Vishwamitra made Ram a great warrior, Guru Sandipan made Krishna a great warrior, Parshuram made Bhishma a great warrior, Surya made Hanuman a great warrior, Aristotle made Alexander, Chanakya made Chandra Gupta. Sometimes teachings are given according to the country, the gurus and time. That is why gurus are considered as being equal to God.

Omkar Swami is a great knowing being. He had once been a professor of medical science. And given many lectures in the military academy. He was a well wisher of the country and was a trikallagya.

He looked minutely at Parth and said, "Dear Parth, this is not the time for you to take sanyas, there are some duties from your last birth that you have to fulfill. PArth said, "God, who was I in my previous birth? What work is left?"Omkar Swami told him that he should lie down in 'Shav Asan' (Dead Pose) and look into his eyes. Parth looked into his eyes and started feeling unconscious and gradually passed out. He felt as if he was flying in the air and had gone to his past birth. What are you looking at now?

He is a member of the Shukla family in Kanpur and his name is Arjun Shukla.

This story of reincarnation is set in Kanpur, one of the important cities of India. Chowk Sarafa is considered the heart of the city. There are shops of silver and gold. On the east side there are shops selling stationery, a masjid and many temples-Koteshwar dham, Krishna Radha, Hanuman temple, etc. Fruit shops and flower shops, on the Western side is Meston Road where there are shops selling leather articles and the population is mainly Muslim, in the North is To[I Bazar. There are many lanes and alleys connected to mohallas. On the South is Hotel Tilak, whole sale shops and a jewellery shop by the name of Shukla Brothers. The shop is owned by Mr. Somnath and he is known as the king of Maharaj ganj. The government has appointed him as a honorary Magistrate.

He has a very big bungalow in Civil Lines. There is a big gate and a big lawn and a big hall. There are two rooms that are even bigger than the hall. The cupboards in the Drawing room are full of books and another one contains beautiful ornaments.

Somnath's family consists of his son Arjun who is very good in studies and had completed his Inter with the PCM group. He was preparing to give the entrance examination of Engineering Colleges. He had obtained

72% in his inter exams and had passed the examination of Roorkee Civil Engineering and Pilani Mechanical Engineering. Arjun's mother did not want to send him away from Kanpur and that is why he had taken admission in B.Sc. 1st year in DAV College. The family decided that he should become an engineer.

Somnath told him to join coaching and Arjun agreed to it. Somnath used to be very busy with his work and could not pay much attention to Arjun. Money was not a problem and they often used to talk about Arjun's future.

It was the month of November and pleasantly cold. A cool breeze was blowing. Somnath, his wife and Arjun were sitting in the hall and the time was around 6 in the evening. Arjun was wearing a blue colored suit. The Maharaj came and put a tray containing tea and biscuits and 'pakodas' on the table. Shanti poured the tea in the cups and gave one cup to Somnathji. She said to Arjun, to have some 'pakodas' and passed him the plate. Arjun took some. The telephone rang and Somnath picked up the phone. The voice at the other end said that he was Dr. Singh speaking from the Medical College and that he had to go to Gwalior the next day and he had forgotten to pick up the ornaments from Somnath's shop. He wanted them to be sent to his home.

Somnath noted down the address which was 14, 1st Floor, D Colony Medical College. Somnath told him that he would send his son Arjun with the ornaments and he told Arjun to call the driver. The driver entered the room and was told to go to the shop and tell Munimji to give the ornaments that had been made in the name of the Doctor and to take them to the doctor's house. He also gave instructions to him to buy some good quality sweets from the sweet shop and take that also. He then called out to Arjun and told him to take the ornaments and the sweets when the Munimji arrived from the shop. Arjun understood what had been told to him and started for the Doctor's house with the ornaments. He reached the gates of the College in half an hour and the college campus was alight with the bulbs placed there at regular distances. The driver stopped the car and asked the address of Dr. B.N. Singh from a medical student. The student guided the car to the house of the doctor. Arjun got down from the car and on reading the information panel he found the location of the house. The driver parked the car to one side and Arjun climbed up the stairs to the house. He pressed the doorbell and could hear the ring echoing inside the house.

The door opened after two minutes and a young beautiful girl was standing in front of him. Arjun told her that he had come to meet the doctor and she went back inside and came back after two-three minutes and asked him to sit in the drawing room. After some time a servant came with two glasses of water in a tray. He took the briefcase from the Munimji. The doctor came and Arjun stood up to greet him. He pressed the bell and asked the servant to bring tea and something to eat. The servant got tea and biscuits and before the Doctor could pour the tea, Arjun got up and did the needful.

They started talking and after drinking the tea Arjun took out the ornaments from the briefcase and kept it on the table. The doctor called out to his daughter Subhadra and told her to bring her mother also.

After some time Subhadra and the doctor's wife came and sat down. Arjun greeted them and his eyes met Subhadra's and they both stared at each other for a long time.

The Munimji took out the necklace, the earring and the chain from the box and showed them. The doctor and his wife looked at the things one by one and Subhadra looked at the ring and started wearing it on her ring finger. Arjun interrupted her and said that it should be worn on the little finger. Subhadra asked him the reason and he told her that since it was embedded with an emerald, it should be worn on the little finger. Emerald is a gemstone of Mercury so it should be according to astrology it worn on the little finger. The doctor held out his right hand and asked Arjun to tell him the importance of each one. Arjun told him that the middle finger represented the sun, the index finger represented Venus the thumb the diamond. One should wear the Gomed for pacifying Rahu, and a nine gemstone ring for all the planets.

The doctor asked Arjun how he had so much knowledge about gemstones. Arjun replied that Umashankar Shastri who used to sit in the shop was a great astrologer and he used to tell Arjun about them, so he knew a little bit of astrology. The doctor asked him whether he knew how to read hands and he said that he knew that also a little bit. He asked his wife and daughter whether the ornaments were ok, his wife's ring was a little tight so it was given to Arjun so that he could get it fitted. The mother asked Arjun what he was doing and he replied that he was studying in B.Sc. first year with PCM as his subjects and was studying in DAV College. It came to be known that Subhadra was also doing B.Sc. with Biology from the same college. Arjun said that he would bring the ring the next day but the doctor told him that he could give it to Subhadra the next day in the college itself. So it was decided that they would meet in the Library in the fifth period that was the Chemistry period. Arjun took leave of them and came home.

He was thinking of Subhadra; the more he tried to turn away his thought from her, the more his thoughts drifted towards her. He kept lying awake at night and got up at 6 o'clock the next day, instead of his usual 5 o'clock. He had a quick breakfast and was waiting for Munimji to arrive with the ring. Then his mother told him that he had already come and given the ring and it was there in the drawer. He quickly took it out and asked his mother for some money. His mother, Shanti gave him two ten rupee notes that he happily took and calling her the best mother he went away to his college. His mother told him that she would cook his favorite dish. When he reached his college, the second period had started and he quickly ran to his class.

"May I come in Sir?"

"Yes, come in, but note for future."

"Sorry Sir"

"Ok."

Arjun sat on his seat. Mr. Nigam was teaching Calculus. He said that since the test match was starting on the 13th he would not come for five days. Wouldn't the college announce holidays during the test match? He could not be sure. The Green Park stadium was right in front of the College and the tickets for the match were sold to the students for a concession. Mostly the N.C.C. cadets and students used to watch the match. Despite being open the college seemed to be closed on such days.

The class came to an end and Arjun started waiting for the 5th period. He went to the Library in the 4th period where he met some other friends and they started making plans about their future. They talked about the entrance examinations of Engineering Colleges.

Subhadra Sen was also doing PCM and told Arjun that she had got Chemical Engineering in HBTI. Arjun congratulated her. She thanked Arjun and asked him what he had in mind. He said that he had given the entrance examination and was waiting for the result. She asked him why he had not thought of the medical line to which he replied that he did not have Biology in his Inter and he said that if he fell ill he could have got treated by her to which the others replied that she would have given him a lethal injection and it was good that she had not become a doctor.

"If I had been a doctor, I would have seen Arjun at the end."

"Why, because he would not have given your fees?"

"No, I would have listened to his prattling with no hurry."

The students got embarrassed and went away. The bell for the 5th period rang and Parth quickly came out to give the ring to Subhadra. The class was supposed to be taken in room no. 20 on the first floor. He entered the class and his eyes searched for Subhadra. He could not see her anywhere and he started getting irritated. One of his friends asked him whether he was looking for Subhadra. Suddenly Professor Srivastava and Subhadra entered the classroom together. Subahdra took her seat in the first row in the corner and Arjun sat down on the second seat of the first row. Before the Professor could begin his lecture, Arjun and Subhadra saw each other. They talked in sign language. Professor Srivastava asked him how he was in his class and he replied that some portion had remained. Subhadra asked the professor how he knew Arjun and the professor replied that Arjun was the naughtiest student and had the lowest marks in Chemistry. Subhadra asked him how he had passed. She was told that his marks in Chemistry were comparatively less since he had obtained 90 in Physics. The professor said that Arjun had not studied properly. She said that he had not taught him properly since Suchita Sen ahd got 90 marks. The professor told him to come near and when he came he caught hold of his ears and said that he would twist his ears and wrench them off.

The entire class started laughing, after the class got over Arjun and Subhadra came to the verandah and walked towards the main gate. They started looking for a place where they could talk without being disturbed, they went to the canteen where a cabin was made where four people could sit and chat. The cabin had curtains in it. They came and the bearer came and brought two glasses of water and the menu. Arjun pushed the menu towards Subhadra.

"Tell me, what should we order?"

"Whatever you like."

They placed an order for two 'dosas' and two coffees.

Arjun gave the ring to Subhadra.

Subhadra said, "Wont you put it in my finger?"

"You know what that means?"

"I am not so naïve."

"What are you saying, a ring is just a gift."

"It means acceptance."

"I am ready for that."

"What will your family say?"

"It does not mean that our marriage is being fixed."

"Why don't you say that you are feeling embarrassed."

"It is not that."

"Then put this ring on my finger.."

Arjun looked carefully at the ring; meanwhile the bearer had come with the two dosas and two types of chutneys-red and green.

Arjun took Subhadra's right hand in his left one and slipped the ring on her little finger. He felt his touch to be like an electric current running through her entire body and Subhadra also liked his touch.

The next day it came to be known that the Chemistry professor had left for the USA. The class for the 'Maths group' students and the Biology groups students would be held together, and this was great news for Arjun and Subhadra. They both sat together for the class and gradually they became very close and started developing feelings for each other.

Since the course was running behind schedule, extra classes started being held on Sundays by Dr. Shrivastava. The first class lasted for two hours. Subhadra and Arjun came out and since the car hd not come to take Subhadra she waited for long. Eventually she thought of going to a public booth and had started going there when her feet suddenly tripped over a stone lying on the way and she lost her balance and fell down. Arjun saw her fall and came running and gently picked her up. She was wincing with pain. Arjun took her to a nearby gazebo and ran to get his car. Subhadra was in a great pain; aRjun told her to be brave and he got the car. He helped her lie down on the back seat and started for Dr. Raj's clinic. Subhadra objected saying that she wanted to go home but Arjun convinced her that since her feet was bleeding he would take her to the doctor first. Subhadra was worried that her parents would wonder where she had gone Dr Raj was well known to Arjun's family, he drove there in ten minutes and on reaching he called out to the compounder who helped him bring down Subhadra from the car and took her to the base of the stairs. Arjun carried her up the stairs and made her sit down in a chair. The doctor was in his cabin attending to patients and the compounder started giving first aid to Subhadra. He wiped the blood with cotton and bandaged it after putting medicine on it. Subhadra was still feeling the pain and Parth told her to be calm and strong. The compounder came and said that the doctor was free.

Dr. Raj was sitting in his cabin and there was a telephone on his table and a paper weight. He had a stethoscope around his neck, near him was a stretcher on which the patients were made to lie down for a check up. Dr.

Raj was sitting in his revolving chair and had to move around from left to right. At his back was a screen where X-rays used to be hung. Dr. Raj was a well known doctor of the district. He was a good natured and soft-spoken person and had a very natural manner. He used to see around 200-300 patients daily and people said that the doctor had a magical touch that healed the patients.

Arjun took Subhadra inside the doctor's cabin, the doctor gestured to Subhadra to sit on the stool. Arjun helped her and gently made her sit on it, it was clear form Subhadra's face that she was in great pain.

When the doctor came to know her address he was astonished and said that it was the address of Dr. V.N. Singh. Subhadra told him that he was her father. He said that he was his guru and asked her how she had got injured. Subhadra told him that her right leg had struck against a brick that made her fall down and twist her ankle. The doctor asked her whether there was any pain in movement or walking. He prescribed some medicines and told her to take them and she would be relieved of the pain. Arjun was given the slip and told to get an X-ray done since there could be a fracture and bone dislocation. Subhadra said that she would go home and get the X-ray done. The doctor told her that it was required urgently so she rang up her home and told her mother that she would be late in coming since she had sustained an injury. Her mother said that she would send the car to fetch her but Subhadra said that Arjun was with her and that he would drop her home. Arjun got her X-ray done from a nearby pathology center and then went back to Dr. Raj. The doctor put the X-ray on his screen and told her that there was no need to get hassled, it was only a slight fracture and he was doing a temporary plaster that would be removed after three days. When Arjun asked him the fee amount he smiled and said that first Subhadra should get well and the there was no hurry for paying the fee. Subhadra expressed her thanks

It was eight o'clock at night and the shops were closing and traffic was gradually thinning. Arjun said that he would take her to his house but Subhadra refused saying that her parents would be worried and that she would come some other time. Arjun brought the car and with the compounder's help put her in the back seat and started driving the car slowly. They reached Subhdra's house in 15 minutes. Arjun told Subhdara to sit till he came back with someone. On getting down he saw a doctor standing there and asked for his help to get Subhadra out of the car. The doctor readily agreed and on seeing Subhadra recognized her. He immediately arranged for a stretcher and took her to her flat where

Subhadra's mother was waiting. Makin Subhadra lie on the bed, Arjun sat down on a chair. The mother sat down near Subhadra and started caressing her forehead.

Arjun gave her a description of the day's events and she blessed him lovingly. Subhadra had started feeling drowsy and she nodded off to sleep. Arjun took his leave. Subhadra's mother saw him off. On reaching his house he went to his room since he was very tired. His mother came into the room and asked him the reason for coming home so late. He expressed his unwillingness to eat and quietly lay down on the bed. He could not sleep since his mind was occupied with thoughts of Subhadra. The more he tried to dispel the thoughts; the more his mind went towards her. Not only was he dwelling on her physical attributes but also on her endearing behavior. His mind told him that he wanted to be near her forever.

Arjun started appearing for the Engineering Entrance examinations for which he studied hard. When his father asked him about his studies he said that they were going ok. Then his father asked him about Subhadra and Arjun told him about her fracture and how it would take a month for her to get better.

His father told him to look after her. He started making notes of the Chemistry lectures and give them to Sunanda.

One day he reached her house with the notes and a box of sweets. There were two more days for her plaster to be opened and she had all medical facilities.

Arjun rang the doorbell of her house and a woman cam out and asked him his name. After some time she asked Arjun to come inside and took him to a room. Subhadra was lying on a bed. Arjun asked her how she was and she replied that she had fallen back in her studies. He told her not to worry since he had brought Chemistry notes for her, to which she replied how she would obtain Biology and Botany notes. Arjun told her that he had asked Suchita Sen and she would give them. Tea was served and Arjun started sipping his tea. The conversation continued.

Subhadra's mother said, "You should become a doctor."

"Aunty, I haven't taken Biology and my family wants me to become an Engineer.

Subhadra, "You do your Inter Biology privately and I am sure that you will clear your PMT examinations."

"How?"

 Sacrificed Life

"See, you are good at Physics and Chemistry and even if you get less marks in Biology, they will be averaged out. There is still time, fill up the forms."

"Who will teach me Biology?"

Subhadra kept her hands on her chest and said that she would teach him. Arjun laughed and said "What will be my tuition fee?"

"Give it to me when you pass." "When I give the PMT examination, you can teach me Physics."

"Ok, done." This was a turning point in Arjun's life.

Arjun filled up the form and also got an opportunity to keep meeting Subhadra. When Subhadra taught him Biology they got the chance to laugh and tease each other. Arjun scored 65 in Biology and passed the examination.

The next year both of them passed the medical examination, and the process of admissions began. Subhadra took admission in the first year of MBBS. Arjun would also have joined MBBS but he contacted jaundice and so he took admission in the second year of B.Sc. The doctor had advised him complete bed rest for three months.

Arjun became very weak but he managed to clear his B.Sc. second year with less marks, but since his marks in the first year were very good, he got a first class. Meanwhile Subhadra's father became the dean of the Gwalior Medical College. Subhadra had cleared her first year of MBBS. Dr. Singh had to shoulder the post of the dean by the 10th of July. Subhadra was worried about Arjun and decided to go to his house. Arjun's mother received her lovingly and offered her some snacks.

As soon as Arjun entered the room they exchanged notes about the last eight months and Arjun said that his dream of becoming a doctor was now shattered. Subhadra consoled him saying that her father had become the principal of Gwalior Medical College and in M.P. admissions ere conducted on the basis of merit. She said that it was good that he had done Biology and that she had brought the forms for MBBS and she was sure that he would be selected. Arjun hugged her and said that she was great.

Subhadra liked his embrace and she gave herself up to him but then Arjun remembered that what he was doing was wrong and said that he was extremely sorry.

Subhadra told him to attach two testimonials and get them attested, but then told him that she would get it done from her father and get the character certificates also made. She told Arjun to get the migration done after he got selected.

Subhadra's family shifted to Gwalior. Dr. Singh was the dean of the College and had got all amenities at home. Subhadra got the form submitted and since he had adequate marks he was selected but on some conditions. He received the news of his admission and was elated Actually, he had not wanted to become a doctor but a successful Civil Engineer but had followed in the footsteps of Subhadra. He had always aspired to be an army officer or an Engineer .Now he was wondering if his father would allow him to go to Gwalior or not. He was also getting admission in Roorkee Engineering college and in Physics. S

Omnath wanted that his son should sit in the shop and manage the business because he had a lot of knowledge about the shop since he used to spend his spare time there. He showed his horoscope to Pandit Umashankar Shastri by calling him to the Sanskrit School that was in the 'Sarafa'. The PAndit was well known for his correct predictions. It was his habit to take some water in his mouth and from a 'lota' and also for reciting mantras in a different voice. He came to the shp after about two hours. Somnath ji got up and touched his feet. He requested him to partake of some sweets which the Pandit did. He ate two 'pedas' and had some water and wiped his lips on a towel.

"Yes, Som, why have you called me?"

"Shastriji, have a look at Arjun's horoscope."

Taking the horoscope, and counting on his fingers the Shastri said

" The boy is very blessed –he will become either an engineer or doctor or a top grade scientist."

"Will he live with us?"

"No."

"He will live away from the house. There are strong chances of his going abroad. There are chances of a love marriage. His wife will be a famous scientist."

Arjun expressed his desire to become a doctor and after taking the advice of well- wishers it was decided that if that was his wish, he should pursue it.

Arjun started packing his things to go to Gwalior. His mother packed eatables for him and both parents went to leave him to the station. When the train left both had tears in their eyes.

But at the same time they were happy with the thought that their son was going to become a doctor.

A new incident after 6 years

The day came when Arjun finally got his degree from the Gwalior Medical College. He had also got selected for M.D. since he had obtained 90% marks in his MBBS. Meanwhile there was some demand from Oxford University and talented doctors were being invited to conduct research on viruses and bacteria.

Arjun and Subhadra started living in two separately allotted flats. Subhadra's parents were on the lookout for a suitable match for her, but were not able to find one. They were worried Subhadra and Arjun were living together but neither had proposed to the other for marriage., they continued living as friends.

When they were together everyone used to consider them as an ideal couple. They used to have their meals together and even lived in the same room but there was no physical relationship between them. One day they decided to go for a movie. Subhadra had to go somewhere so she said that she would reach directly and Arjun should go. Arjun agreed to this plan. Subhadra reached the theatre exactly at 6.00. An English movie was going on, she kept waiting but Arjun did not turn up. Eventually, she came back to the flat and saw a lock hanging on the door. She was unlocking the door when the neighbor told her that the operation of Dr. Mehta's son had been suddenly decided upon and Dr. Arjun had to go for it. She cooled down a bit and thought that doctors had a difficult life to live.

It was eleven at night. The bell rang and Arjun was standing there, neither of them spoke. Arjun asked her whether she had eaten and she said that she never ate alone. Arjun said that she should have eaten. Subhadra asked him if he had eaten and he lied that he had. Since they were not very hungry they had some bread slices with butter and coffee and then came and lay down on the bed.

Subhadra's anger had not totally died down. Even when Arjun said sorry and held his ears she did not give any reaction. It was eleven at night and there was total silence.

Subhadra asked him how the operation had been and Arjun told her that it had been successful. Arjun told her one incident from Dr. Raj Kapoor's life. Dr. Raj Kapoor was a doctor who was very busy and found it difficult to take time out for his wife. Once his wife asked him to accompany her for a movie and he agreed but he could not make it and said sorry to his wife. Another time she said that she had got the tickets and that she was waiting in the car and he should come down and join her. When he did not come for a long time she got down from the car and found a crowd of people outside the dispensary. When she enquired she was told that a boy had consumed poison and the doctor was treating him. She went back to her room. The doctor treated the boy and saved his life and his family expressed their gratefulness to him. The doctor was a very easy-going and kind hearted person.

Subhadra was listening very intently and asked, "What was Mrs. Raj's reaction?"

"When she came to know the truth, she cooled down and felt proud of her husband."

Subhadra showed renewed interest and said, "Arjun, how do you know so much?"

I also lived in the same colony. People used to stand there just to have a look of him. He was six foot tall and his wife was also 5.9. Both had glowing skin and were very popular with people. Subhadra remembered that it was Dr. raj who had treated her seven years back.

Arjun told her that he had seen many ups and downs in their life. Then Raj told her that he was talking about Dr. Raj's second wife.

"Did his first wife leave him or did she die?"

Before he could reply, the telephone rang, he picked up the receiver and came to know that he had to reach Kanpur without delay since his father wanted him to be there.

It is the rule of materialistic division that the sum parts of a whole should be equal to one, otherwise the division will be considered as faulty.

It is this faulty division that gives rise to struggle and later assumes the form a destructive war. When rights are violated and tyrants make wrong use of their armed forces, terrorism is born and the clouds of destruction hover above us. Communist countries turn into ruins and then their arrogant faces come to the fore. PArth roars that he wants his portion of the sky and his voice echoes all around and a great war begins.

Shri Krishna again brings the proposal of peace but the greediness of countries makes them blind and then begins another Mahabharat.

Ram-Ravana, Krishna-Kans, Moosa Phirona again take form and this story continues without any end.

Arjun reached his home. He came to know that his parents had fixed his marriage without his consent. He was astounded. What should he do now? His brother Parth had been adopted by his father's elder brother and was the heir to his real father's wealth. There had never been any dispute regarding wealth. Parth had done MSW and was running an NGO and had a lot of respect in society.

Somnath and his wife told Arjun that the girl they had selected was very beautiful and a graduate and was the daughter of the king of Maharaj Nagar and her name was Rajni. They showed her photograph to Arjun, he looked at it without much interest and wanted to tell about Subhadra but could not bring himself to do it.

The date had also been fixed, Arjun told his parents that he was going to get his things from Gwalior. His father said that it was not required but Arjun said that it was very important.

His father told him to stay in Kanpur and practice.

Arjun talked to Parth and made him aware of the circumstances, "Brother, you are so intelligent, please save me."

"Why don't you say no?"

"I don't have the courage."

"Then get married."

Both of them made a plan. They both started out for the market. Parth dropped Arjun to the station from where he took a train to Gwalior; Arjun had given a letter to Parth to be given to his parents.

When they read the letter they were astounded. They wondered what to do; the Raja Saheb had given them advance money in the form of dowry and Somnath was worried about his social standing. It crossed his mind that he should ask Parth to marry the Raja's daughter. He talked to Parth and his younger brother and asked Raja Saheb for some time to be given to him. The Raja sahib said that he was the daughter's father and had his place in society. Everyone knew that his daughter was getting married to the honorary Magistrate Somnath's son.

Arjun got married to Subhadra in a court. After that Arjun's parents got them married as per the rituals and rites. The entire Gwalior turned up to wish the newly-weds. Both of them were very happy. Both were doing biological research. When Arjun's research paper was published he immediately got a fellowship of the U.S. IT was a matter of great pride. The name of Gwalior Jivajirao University shone bright on the horizon. Major countries had made laboratories and were getting the research done according to their own standards. Some countries were flouting the norms of the WHO.

In Belgium research was going on in the field of the possible use of sensory brain. In these trials in Gant University, the model of the brains of 25 tumor patients and 11 control units was made by using the sensory brain technique. They found that the software could make accurate predictions about the effects of the tumour. It is hoped that in the future ....

Memory is one of the most complex processes of the brain. Memory is a collection of information and its retrieval in the future. For any living being to function normally it is extremely important that it has the capability to store and retrieve it efficiently.

The recent studies carried out buy the researchers of Los Angeles University in the leadership of David L. Glangeman show that memory is transferred from one living being to another in the form of RNA. Before this, in the decade of 1940 it was shown by the psychologist of Canada, Donald Heb, that there is a connection between memory neutrons and when this connection becomes strong and are present in large amounts, memory gets stored.

The question was what sort of medicines should be given before and after surgery and the main point was to develop special types of medicines so that the brain of the surgeon and staff could be kept normal during special circumstances so that they could work continuously for ten hours without getting tired. Arjun was invited by the Bonn University of Germany for this purpose. He had received many offers from different countries.

He had signed a contract with Oxford University for two years. Meanwhile, Dr. Subhadra had completed her M.S. She had become a professor in Jivaji Rao University. Dr. Arjun decided to call Dr. Subhadra to work with him and Oxford University gave him permission to call her.

Dr. Arjun was doing research on viruses. It was spreading fast and had even spread among the soldiers. Dr. Arjun had earlier also worked on viruses because of which he got early success in making its vaccine. The medicine was also made that could control the virus in one week, and Arjun's reputation in the medical world increased. It was even being said that he could make dead people come alive. The British government awarded him the post of a Captain in the army for the treatment of infectious diseases.

In his letter Dr. ARjun has written in detail that he was working on an antidote for the virus and for a person to survive without food for a long time and that he had achieved success. The trails on animals had been successful and plans were afoot to carry out human testing. But the research had been kept a secret.

Legends create curiosity, but sometimes there is a grain of truth to them. One such story had been provided by a security guard.

Abduction

All the newspapers carried the headlines of the abduction of researcher Dr. Arjun from the Oxford Unevrsity. The Indian Embassy immediately charged the British government of being lax about the matter. Opposition parties raised questions about the security lapse.

The British government immediately handed over the case of Dr. Arjun's abduction to the Secret Intelligence Service, SIS and MI6. IT also asked the US for help. America immediately alerted the FBI and the MI and Interpol also joined in the operations.

The newspapers were printing the news in different ways and the British government was getting maligned. Nobody knew whose handiwork this was. The Indian government handed over the investigation to the IB although some days earlier the IB had given the report that scientists were in danger, especially those doing biological research. The UN had imposed sanctions on chemical war. The government said that it could not rule out the hand of terrorist organizations. The security agencies were doing their work. In such a situation the Indian government provided security to the families of Dr. Arjun and Dr. Subhadra and the secret cells were keeping an eye on them. But no clue could be found.

Dr. ARjun had been imparted special military training by the British government and also trained in using arms under martial arts. He was capable of saving himself under all circumstances. The members of MI6 reached the laboratory and probed the security guard.

"What time did Dr. Arjun come to the laboratory?"

"At 1.10."

"Did he come at the same time everyday?"

"No."

"Then what time did he come?"

"At 11.00."

"What was the reason for coming late that day?"

"Was he was with someone that day?"

"No,."

"What time did he leave the laboratory?"

"Sir, actually there was no time for going back, but normally he used to go around 6.00."

"Did you see any suspicious person around?"

"At what time did he leave that day?"

"Sir, he didn't come out that day."

"How is that possible, show the register."

It was true, there was no signature showing his departure. That meant that the abduction had taken place from the laboratory itself.

Dilemma and victory over self

Parth got married to the daughter of Maharaj Nagar, Nisha, with great pomp and show. Parth was the adopted son of his father and he was also the heir to his father's wealth. He also had a share in Somnath's property. His in-laws wanted that Arjun's portion should also be given to Parth. They started hatching and plotting in order to achieve this end. Arjun was not in India; whatever he had was his own earning but he was entitled to his share of the property. Parth was not at all greedy, he had a lot of respect for his brother, but his in-laws were pestering him. Nisha was also working in an NGO that was working in various fields. His daily routine was getting affected and he told his friends about it. One of them suggested that he should go on a pilgrimage for some days. Looking at his circumstances he felt that there were three stages of money-use, donation and destruction. IF money was used for the welfare of human beings one's life was successful. Thinking about these things he decided that he should go on a tour of the far- flung undeveloped villages He began his tour and he started studying various temples, masjids, gurudwaras and churches.

In his study he found that inhuman acts were enacted here and double personalities were also common. These places of worship had unlimited funds and history is witness to the fact that aggressors have looted these places for their selfish gains.

He started ruminating on the plight of the helpless people and thought that such a city should be created where people of all castes could reside and work together.

He began holding discussions with prominent personalities of all religions and castes. He recalled that ashrams had been made by the best sant mahatmas of India. He had read that from whichever lanes sants passed, their positive energies got dispersed in the environment there and the place used to become sacred and the people of those areas began thinking of human welfare. He was given an area of 10 square kilometers on lease for a term of ten years and was assured of government support. Some countries believe in Vastrushastra, some don't.

PArth invested the entire portion of Arjun's money in this project. Plans do not work out on the basis of mere dreams, one had to make efforts in order to give practical form to them and the government decided to think on this matter once again.

Indian and foreign architects were called and maps were made. The area was developed in the form of a square. There would be four entrances and the fifty storeys would be 50 in number and have all facilities. There would be a distance of 40 meters between each building with a concrete track. There would be parks, exercise rooms, gyms, swimming pools, play grounds for children, banks, etc and a market in each building so that essential items were easily available. Besides this there would be two theatres, a temple, a masjid, a church, a gurdwara and a beautiful hall for the Brahma worshippers and a very big water tank. There would be about 100 huts in the North The construction would be such that included the preamble of the constitution.

We are all born will seek dreams & have a lifetime to shape our dreams into reality.

The Preamble

We the people of India having solemnly resolved to constitute India into a sovereign, socialist, secular, democratic Republic and to secure to all citizens Justice- Social, Economic and Political.

Liberty of Thought, expression, belief, faith & worship.

Equality of status & of opportunity and to promote among them all

Fraternity-assuring the dignity of individual and the unity and integrity of the nation in our constituent assembly this twenty sixth day of November 1949 do hereby adopt enact and give to ourselves this constitution.

The soul of the Indian constitution is inherent in this and the construction of Arjun Nagar began on this basis.

Parth had understood his duty and he stopped the storm of selfish motives that were raging inside him. He established himself as a shining star in the international arena.

But he was facing criticism too. Worries were being expressed about the present and past incidents. The king of Maharaj Nagar and Nisha were opposing him. They wanted that only Hindus should be given residences there. They were encouraging an anti-Muslim rhetoric. It was being said that Muslim rulers were against Hindus and India was also affected by this mentality.

The city was given the name of Arjunpur. It was a mini India, PArth had given form to his imagination with his positive efforts and he was being praised by most people but some were proving him to be anti-national.

Maharaj Sahab was in favor of making a Hindupur and was also an opponent, he gave rise to a new dispute. He challenged that it was the land of Hindus and their forefathers. He asked whether there were temples in Muslim countries and if not then why.

PArth said, "There are temples in Sharjah and in Saudi Arabia and I don't want to talk on this subject."

"Why don't you want to talk?"

"There is no reply to every 'why'. We accept all religions in the world; if Islam considers itself to be the best that is its opinion. Arjun has his own opinion and there is no compromise with the fact that Arjun Nagar will be made here."

It was constructed with all facilities and amid a friendly ambience. A new idea where people of all faiths were there-Pandit, maulvi, granthi and pujari. Parth, you are great!

The raja sahib was actually opposing it because he wanted Arjun's property to come to his daughter Nisha, but Parth's brotherly love had foiled his attempts. Parth had repeated the story of Ram and Bharat. PArth felt mentally satisfied but he could not sleep till late. Thoughts flitted in his mind-the working of the mind is actually a mystery. He had once read Modern who had written that one cannot imagine a world without a villain. It is only a person's will that saves him from all difficult situations. He saw a dream that Arjun was making a cure for human welfare in a laboratory in some University. When he got up in the morning the news in large letters in many newspapers was that the great scientist Dr. Arjun had been abducted.

Underground terrorist groups were very much surprised about the identity of the organization that had abducted Dr. Arjun. They suspected each other of it, the needle of suspicion was strongly indicating the hand of the Islamic State. It was suspected that the Islamic state and Boko Haram had together executed the abduction.

Dr. Arjun had prepared an anti-virus against some virus. The anti-virus acted against the virus and killed it and increased the body's immunity. This news had been given by many newspapers. After that the news started getting censored. A ban was imposed on any interview given by Dr. Arjun.

Arjun wrote to the Indian government and talked to Dr. Subhadra who was very worried. Ian Indian team of the IB and CBI left for London. The ambassador of India was given the entire story. The situation in India became very tense. The officials of the CBI and the IB held secret meetings with Indian officials. The news was obtained by the F.B.I. America is a friend of India and its showed its sympathy and assured help.

The government of the U.K. made plans of bringing Dr. Subhadra by plane. The secret meeting of Dr. Subhadra, and the officials of the CBI and the IB was arranged in an underground hall. Discussions were under way on the research papers prepared by Dr. Arjun. Dr. Arjun had written a chapter on chemical war. For example the chemical war of Russia on Syria, of China on Korea and some other nations but none of the countries had accepted the allegations and neither had they been proved. Although the terror organizations do not have any power, their rule still reigns supreme. They were making efforts to make chemical weapons and that is why they had abducted Dr. Arjun. The Chinese government also had a hand in it.

One cannot imagine the depths to which the Chinese can fall in order to come out trumps in the war of supremacy. They snatched away Tibet by deceiving Pandit Nehru in the name of the Pansheel pact and the Dalai lama had to take refuge in India during the 1962 war.

There is a very big laboratory in Wuhan city of china. The astonishing fact is that it has received huge amount of funds from America. Many countries indirectly violate the orders of the United Nations and the danger of world war remains because of the narrow mentality of some countries.

When the secret meeting took place, the truth emerged. A terror organization was going to carry out the abduction of Dr. Arjun at the instance of some country. The MI6 was informed when the organization reached the laboratory for carrying out the abduction.

Dr. Arjun was sent underground. He became infected with the same virus that he was working on. When it was decided to complete the half done research it became known that Dr. Subhara was working on the same virus and that is why she had been secretly called to carry on the research. Dr. Arjun was secretly kept in a hospital where a team of expert doctors were treating him. Everyone breathed a sigh of relief.

Dr. Subhadra and Parth were secretly taken to a hospital where Dr. Arjun was being treated. They were made to wear special clothes as precaution. The ward was on the 4th floor of O.S.hospital in London; nobody could go there without the special permission of the government.

Initially Dr. Arjun seemed physically weak; he talked to PArth and Dr. Subhadra. Dr. Subhadra's eyes were filled with tears and asked him why he had come here when he was facing no problem in India.

Every person has a mission and dream but one has to sacrifice a lot. I lost some and won something is the rule of nature. Dr. Subhadra mentioned about the property in India and said that he should think about it. Dr. Arjun replied that he was getting a good package and a royalty from books. He had an income of lakhs and was donating to voluntary organizations-all these were things that gave a meaning to life and said that Parth would take care of the property in India.

Dr. Subhadra returned to the laboratory from where she had to gather information about Dr. Parth. She took his case history from Dr. Louis who was treating him. She made a deep study and became a part of the same team.

Arjun was very happy on learning the entire story of the establishment of Arjun Nagar from Parth and blessed him. Arjun said that he had only one objective and that was to keep his country safe from terrorists and to change governments that made wrong policies. Parth said that it was a difficult task, Arjun replied that he would do it even if he had to be reborn.

The time for meeting patients was over. Parth returned to India and the inauguration of ARjun Nagar was done by the Chief Minister of the State. In about a year's time about one lakh people of every caste started living there.

Subhadra's loyalty towards her husband

Dr. ARjun got the feeling that his end was near. His mind became diverted towards God and it was self inspired. He regularly chanted the name of Ram which gave him a lot of peace. He had done his education through English medium so he started reading the English translation of religious texts. Whatever be the language it is an expression of God.

Dr. Subhadra began a research on the virus that had attacked Dr. Arjun. She appointed many doctors as her assistants and formed a team of specialized doctors.

The research work began. Looking after Dr. Arjun and being immersed in research work became Dr. Subhadra's daily routine. Reading various scientific books and consulting various specialists on the subject. Experiments are sometimes successful, at other times they fail. Dr. Arjun and Dr. Subhadra would talk and laugh. Dr. Arjun had become weak, one day Dr. Subhadra told him that she would cure him totally otherwise she would burn herself on his funeral pyre. Dr. Arjun laughed very loudly at this and Subhadra asked him what was so funny. Arjun said that he remembered his great-grand mother's story and started relating it.

'Subhadra, my great-grandfather was a military officer, one day my great-grand mother got up early in the morning and adorned herself. Everyone looked at her in astonishment. She told everyone that he had become a martyr.

Everyone was surprised since there was no communication in those days. The news spread in the entire village and after half an hour the body of my great grandfather actually arrived in the village. A large crowd gathered and his hearse was decorated. My great grandmother went to the crematorium despite everyone's wishes. While everyone else was crying, she was very calm. The legal ban on Sati was the result of the efforts of Raja Ram Mohun Roy. Earlier widows were forcibly made to become 'satis', but then this practice came to an end, but one gets instances of women becoming satis of their own free will.

"You make fun of the practice of Sati."

"Oh no, in fact you should marry again after I die. I allow."

"What nonsense!"

From then on the lamp of Sati Devi is lighted in our family on all auspicious occasions."

Dr. Arjun became disease-free with Subhadra's efforts. They again started going out together and having fun. Dr. Arjun and Dr. Subhadra went around in a car roaming the streets of London. They did a lot of shopping, went to a restaurant and ate to their heart's content.

After leaving the restaurant, they drove around and went home late at night.

Their car suddenly overturned and both had to be admitted to a hospital. Dr. Arjun was in a critical state and he was in the I.C.U. Dr. Subhadra was also in a semi-conscious state.. Dr. Arjun's life came to an end and Dr. Subhadra had been badly wounded. The death of Dr. Arjun was kept a secret from her. She was reading the newspaper and drinking her tea when her eye went to the news that the 'Great Scientist Dr. Arjun was no more.' She fell unconscious. When the doctors came they declared her dead and it was as if their talks about Sati had come true.

Parth woke up from a deep sleep and found Om Swami to be near him and telling him that he had to fulfill his previous birth's tasks.

"What are my orders?"

"First of all you have to become strong and face all adverse situations; you should be able to send all information without any device and be able to read a person's forehead-you have to develop all these capabilities within you. And you have to develop the power of staying without food and water for long periods of time."

"Gurudev, all this seems like fairy tales of another universe."

"Dreams take actual form therefore I order you to dream of good things."

"Take me under your auspices." The world is eternal and cannot be understood. Parth was imbued with a host of good qualities and could stay alive as long as he wanted. It had been one month since Parth had been living in the ashram and he was feeling vigorously alive.

Next Birth

Great souls are reincarnated from time to time. Most institutions believe in rebirth. There is no such belief in the Vedas but research is going on.

The belief is that if a person dies with his deepest desires remaining unfulfilled, he is reincarnated for the fulfillment of those desires. This story is repeated endlessly.

Vinayak used to narrate Ram's story to Vandana everyday. Vandana used to think logically but she had faith in Ram. IT is said that whatever thoughts dominate a woman's mind during her pregnancy, the same are passed on to her child. A very beautiful boy was born to her at twelve o clock and it is said by learned men that if a child is born at this hour then there is no need to get his horoscope made. The child born at this time is very lucky.

Arjun had taken birth as the son of Vinay and Vanshika and Parth was the second son. Ram and Laxman were there in the Treta era, Krishna Balram in the Dwapar era. In the Treta era Ram was the elder brother and Laxman was the younger but in the Dwapar era, Laxman and Balram were elder and Ram and Krishna were younger, and same was the case with Arjun-PArth and Parth Arjun. Births take place according to mental tendencies.

   SACRIFICED LIFE

Arjun died because he was eager to fulfill the dreams that he had seen, when PArth came to the ashram of Om Swami he realized that he had been born to fulfill the remaining deeds of his past life. PArth had become free of the fear of death.

Brigadier B.S. Singh did not like PArth. He suspected that the deal of the secret photograph that had been handed over to the enemy country through the medium of IPS Gupta had been uncovered by the Captain and he wanted to remove him from his path and was therefore looking for some excuse. He was thinking of making Colonel Nadeem the scapegoat but since his record was very good he had to think of someone else. His efforts had been unsuccessful once. The entire world is divided into subcontinents. Most of the countries are fighting for a democratic system and each country has its devotees and tyrants. Many terror organizations are patronized by the governments.

The Republic of Chad is a country in Central Africa. Its neighboring countries include Sudan, Cameroun and Nigeria. IT was named after the Chad lake. France had captured it in 1920 and made it a part of French Equatorial Africa. After the war of independence under the leadership of France Tamblbe in August 1960, Chad became free. The Republic of Congo is situated in Central Africa. In the North there is the Central African Republic and Sudan in the South. In the east is Uganda and Burundi in the South, Zambia and Angola in the West and the Atlantic Ocean and the Tanganyika lake in the east Congo has fallen into ruins because of war.

South Africa was facing the issue of Apartheid, the Pretorian government was perpetrating atrocities on the people and Nelson Mandela was rotting in jail. There was no country in this continent where the government was not oppressive.

Governments were facing public dissent. There are ....organizations that have connections with terrorist organizations. An important factor is that the terrorist organizations get the support of the people. European countries have a hidden hand in the terrorist organizations of Asian countries. America has the largest number of offices of terrorists.

When PArth got the history of a terrorist organization called 016 , he thought that it was fighting for the good of human beings. The government of the country was behaving cruelly with the people. The ruler was a tyrant; the group O16 was pleading for help but it was not getting any. The armies of many countries were sent for help; many times the governments keep the information secret.

The tyrant ruler took two school buses of a special group of children to a deserted spot. The children were made to form three rows and the driver was told to maul them down so that they died a tortuous death. This information was received by the O16 group. It was 50 kms far from that place and could not save the children. Captain PArth had met the head of the group in Delhi. He had told PArth that he was an officer of the NDS. Captain Parth had given him a secret mobile number. Captain Parth was just 5 kms away from that place. The NDS officer pleaded with Parth to save the children and said that he would sacrifice his life also but Parth was not to reveal his identity.

CaptainParth used nano-technology. Military was all around the area where the children were being held. There were three tiers of the military. He made a plan of entering the area in the same military dress. He could manage to enter with a fake I.D. and was moving ahead with all precautions.

The O16 group had sent its members. There was a huge ground surrounded by military camps. All the people were armed and some were acting as guards. The tyrant was sitting on a big stage and had military security all around. The children were screaming with nobody to hear them.

The tyrant once again told the driver to finish them all who was pleading with folded hands. The soldiers had made arrangements for torching the bus with their specially loaded revolvers that had a range of 500 meters.

Suddenly a fire broke out in the camps and nobody could comprehend what was happening. The stage was engulfed in smoke.

PArth told the driver to put all the children in the bus and flee from there. Parth had put a rope all around that was causing the explosions; he removed it from one side to let the bus go. He climbed on the top of the bus and started killing the soldiers. The bus reached the main gate. The gate was closed but suddenly there was an explosion and the gate opened immediately. The bus was now out of the camp. PArth had managed to get the buses out safely. Reporters gathered and the people of the O16 group also came. The tyrant got the news censored. The O16 group now salvaged the situation and this was the obligation that they owed to Parth. Its chief had given a fake identity to Parth. He wanted to tell his real identity and ask for forgiveness for the fake ID.

The question before the government was of finding out the name of the organization/person that had been able to break into the security and save the children. The O16 group took the responsibility for this- from time to time the U.N.O. and some countries give out a list of terror organizations and take each other's help to combat terror. It has also been seen that the defense officials, big businessmen and big politicians sell the political strategies for their own selfish gains and the countries are badly destroyed in such instances. In such circumstances those who are in danger of being unmasked, try to get rid of these people and even get them killed.

On the other hand, there are such brave officers who do not sell their integrity for any amount of money, even if they have to lose their lives.

Sometimes the right people in the government do not get the required support and there can be two reasons for this. Either they do not understand the seriousness of the situation or are compelled by some secret pact. An IB officer had written in his report that the brother of the Chief Minister was a smuggler and had a hand in kidnappings. That report was suppressed.

Security

Safety and attack are opposite of each other. Both are essential; it all depends on circumstances. Adverse conditions block our way and struggle opens up paths; not admitting defeat is a good behavior.

There are some people in the defense department who save the country and give up all that they possess.

Captain Parth had been court martialled under a conspiracy. He had become mentally upset. Often people start ignoring you and the question was how to prove himself innocent. For this he needed the help of secret agent IPS Vanshika. There was a communication gap. He could not exchange information because of the presence of a jammer in the area where he was stationed.

One group of the military was happy. They had managed to get the thorns out of the way. The department was worried about how the pictures of secret and restricted places was getting leaked. Cyber crimes were increasing and the Indian government had to reply to questions about cyber crime. Terrorist groups were killing innocent people.

The defense minister had called the chiefs of the army, navy and air force separately and held meetings. All of them said that they wanted an officer who had worked on cyber crime and who had good knowledge of artificial intelligence. He should have a deep understanding of the working style of terrorist organizations. A list of names appeared according to computer generated information. These included colonel Naseem, Major Ashok, Mittal and Captain PArth and some others whose track was not very good. One name was of IPS secret agent, Vanshika also.

It was essential to include Varsha in this team because she had a good experience of working with the public. IT was she who had given the information to the IB that IPS Shrivastava had sold photographs of restricted places to a foreign company and because of Vanshika's intelligence the packet had been switched. The IB had censored the exchange of information between suspected officials. This secret information was obtained by those officials.

Except of Captain PArth and Colonel Naseem nobody had any suspicion on Brigadier B.N. Singh, but they had no proof.

The defense minister called a secret meeting of officers. The meeting lasted for many hours and the personal file of captain PArth was also checked and it was found that he had connections with the O16 terror organization. He had meddled in the work of the South African government. Captain PArth accepted these facts because he did not want to let it be known that he suspected Brigadier B.N.Singh.

The government was compelled to include Captain Parth in this team, it was thinking of returning the commission, Colonel Naseem asked whether it would be proper to do the court martial at this time.

Sir, the information about the court martial is there with terrorist organizations nad the governments of some countries and that is why the enemy has become careless that they have no danger from Captain Parth.

The Indian and American governments were worried where the enemy countries used the OPG portal improperly. This portal exchanges the information between both countries.

The Taliban mounted a terror attack on Afghanistan. The Taliban attacked the embassies of America, Britain and Germany and tried to enter the National Assembly. They attacked 11 places and destroyed the statue of Gautam Buddha with tanks.

America and Phillipines was practicing war because of china's activities and it was given the name of Bali Cotton. 4500 American nad 2300 Phillipine soldiers took part in this exercise. Its objective was to protect the maritime bases of the countries and to control china's challenge over the South china sea and wrong policies of the Chinese.

There was a lot of unrest on the world stage. Most countries were flouting international rules and were working on accumulating atomic power. There were a lot of differences between America and Iran. America was opposing terrorism while China was giving protection to them. India was not left untouched. Even after restrictions on the manufacture of atom bombs and their use, some terrorist organizations and countries were working on it. India's security agencies were alerting that terrorist attacks could take place at any time. Pakistan was giving active support to terrorist organizations and conducting terror camps. This was a well -known fact but China was supporting it clandestinely.

Captain Parth was included in the team. He made a plan to present his facts after meeting Colonel Naseem and other members. The biggest question was how to protect the country. Captain Parth included some activities from his life. One has to go the root of the matter if one has to resolve a problem, although sometimes instant decisions have to be taken, but the outcome can be ....

In the context of local and international level, PArth proposed that deliberations should be held on the main points and the mental outlook of the countries should be taken into account.

Some members were in agreement with him while others were not. PArth said that even thought they were not ready to ponder over the points as yet, they would do so in the future. It was Parth's opinion that funding to the terrorist and extremists should be stopped and their bank accounts should be hacked. The team members were not inclined towards this. They wanted a fake account to be opened and money to be transferred to it. There was danger in this.

In the eyes of the terrorists, India was among the foremost countries in the world. It has its own policies that change according to the situations. In the detailed study that Parth made, he handed over his observations to the government in which he clearly wrote that we could not control terrorism totally as long as we abided by some articles of the Indian Constitution-his indication was towards Kashmir.

Hindus are a class of people who do not believe in violence. It talks of all religions and it also does not mean that all Hindus will be the same. According to Hindu beliefs it is said that we should change according to the times. An important point is the mental make up of the government and the ideology of the opposition and people's philosophy.

Jammu & Kashmir State was established on 26th October 1947. Its summer capital is Srinagar and winter capital is Jammu. The area is 222.36 square kilometers and the population density is 56 per square kilometer. The population of men is 6665561, that of women is 5883365. The Jammu area is 5350811 Kashmir area is 6907622, Ladakh area is 290492, literacy among men is 68.78%, literacy among women is 58.01%, Hindus are 29.3% , Muslims are 66.97%, Sikhs are 2.03% and others are 1.3%. The main languages are Urdu and Dogri.

Geographical situation- IT is the northernmost state of India situated in the Himalayan mountain range. Boundaries are Himachal Pradesh and Punjab in the South, China in the North east, Pakistan occupied Kashmir in the west. The main tourist places here are Vaishno Devi Shrine, Shri Raghunath temple, Ranveereshwar temple, Shiv Khodi, Amarnath dham, Shanakracharya temple etc. The problem of Kashmir is very complex. The scholars and politicians have had different opinions on it. From Pandit Jawaharlal Nehru to Dr. Shyama Prasada Mukherjee to Sardar Vallabhbhai Patel- the opinions on Kashmir have never been the same.

China and Pakistan have been stridently anti India. These two countries are forever trying to spread violence and terrorists run their parallel governments here. The government does not exercise a strong will power.

Parth declared that terrorism could not be contained until article 370 of the Indian Constitution was repealed and article 35A was also referred to. The team wrote to the government that Parth should be removed from the team since he had no proper strategy to combat terrorism.

It was Captain Parth's opinion that since the army's hands were tied, it could not take any decision and it did not have any other alternative but to commit suicide. He clearly wrote that he should be set free. Everyone was praise for his bravery. Wars are not won by governments but by armed forces. His style of working was rejected.

Captain Parth related the history of Kashmir. On 26th October 1947, Maharaj Harising signed the papaers for the break up of the royal state, before this the Dogra kings had ruled and the base was laid down by Maharaja Gulab Singh. Gulab Singh had been anointed by Maharaj Ranjit Singh on the banks of the Chenab on 17th June 1922.

The kingdom could have been divided into three parts-Jammu, Kashmir and Ladakh. Jammu would have been Hindu majorit, Kashmir Muslim majority and Ladakh Buddhist majority state. According to belief the place where Kashmir is situated, there was a huge lake and Jalobdev used to reside there. The entire water of the lake was drunk by Rishi Kashyap and made the land free of the 'daitya' that is why the land is called Kashmir. According to the belief regarding the establishment of Jammu, Raja JAblochan saw a lion and a goat drinking water together. He was influenced by this and set up the place called Jammu.

 Sacrificed Life

Shah Mir was the first Muslim leader of Kashmir. (1399-42) The longest glacier of Karakoram and the second longest glacier of the world (Nan Polar area) and the biggest war area of the world (5753 meters above sea level) Siachen is also here. The major rivers of this area are Chenab, Jhelum and the Sindhu.

Because of the policies of the then government the State has felt the heat of the wars that India has fought after independence- 1947, 1962, 1965, 1971 and 1991.

His eyes well up with tears and he feels like killing those dastardly people in a manner that history ahs not seen before. His eyes become blood-shot. The Hindus of the valley had to be leave the valley in 1990 because of terrorism. The poverty here is 4% that is the least in all of India. The only thought raging in his mind was to get rid of terrorism without thinking of any other rationale. Pakistan was getting aid from the governments of Muslim countries and terror organizations. It was running terror- training camps. Here it is worth noting that America was adopting double standards. Secret pacts with terrorist organizations some where and opposition at other places.

Deliberating on the observations of secret departments is the most important part. IT alerts the country about future crises and gives information about the tiniest bit of happenings in countries. It presents its analysis based on internal and external working systems. And the country prepares its line of defense.

Parth's entire life story is interesting to say the least- from his training to becoming a Captain, from discharging his duties in his home country and abroad, his mission regarding the O16 group, saving the American and Indian armed troops caught in the city of Baghdad from the arms of death for which he had to adopt constitutional and unconstitutional means, but was able to save 200 gallant officers. The verdict was that he was a person with a lot of intelligence, a gallant officer who could go beyond constitutional systems in order to save human lives.

An uncontrolled, undisciplined and law-breaking, slightly insane officer, but who wanted how to destroy cruel governments when he got an opportunity, one who gave his assistance to organizations working for the good of people like Colonel Naseem, and dealing with corrupt people like B.N.Singh even though it meant that he found himself on the other side of the law.

He brought to light the corruption that was rampant in the defense department, but did not make it public. He gave its secret analysis only to the General and the President; the defense minister was not happy with this because they want to spread the politics of caste even in the defense department.

The tyrants of many countries made many plans in order to fulfill their sexual needs. They created armies comprising of beautiful women for this purpose. If they took a fancy to some official's wife, they would get that official killed and make the wife a victim of their lust. The sons or nephews of those tyrants would pass all limits of atrocities. They would openly abduct girls and if anyone opened his mouth he would be killed. Captain Parth guided the terror organizations in some countries and got the governments changed.

There was a crisis when those countries who used to financially help the terror organizations found that the bank accounts of these organizations had been hacked and all the transactions came to a standstill. As a result, terrorist activities were reduced. According to Captain Parth we can control terrorists if we put a stop to all their financial sources.

Terrorism is a big challenge for the United Nations. India was getting criticized and on the other hand it was getting praise; one country was putting allegations on another and the cycle was going on.

Computer hacking comes under cyber crime. A computer hacker is a person who enters into other computer networks illegally. The objective can be financial gain or merely to have some fun, but Parth's intention was to keep an eye on some terrorist organizations and to jam their banking system.

Along with computer studies, Captain Parth had studied information technology. He was thinking that if we were to get control over the terrorists, we would have to think like them and increase our artificial intelligence.

This officer had become a pain in the neck; there were countless charges against him but the ones he had attacked were criminals of the highest order whether they were in the government or normal people.

After the Court Martial he went to meet his girl friend, Nirupama Roy. She was a princess and extremely beautiful. Raj Nagar was situated at the border of West Bengal. Her palace was spread over many acres. And was seven storeys high. There were about a hundred rooms on each floor with balconies and big halls. The king had his own army and a huge cache or arms. He held a lot of influence over the government.

Naxalite activities had grown in the past few years. The Naxalites used to give orders in their own manner and if they were disobeyed they were ordered to be given the death sentence They used to mislead the people and get landlords killed. The Naxalites were beyond the government's reach. No officer wanted to venture into Naxalite areas.

The rule of Raja Sahib was very good. The subjects were taken care of and there were arrangements for schools, hospitals, dharamshalas, haats, etc and the area was one of natural beauty.

Nirupama Roy welcomed Captain Parth and introduced him to her father but did not tell her father that he was a captain in the army because PArth had told her not to. Nirupama took him for a tour of the palace and the nearby areas. There was always a danger of Naxalite attacks in the area.

Captain Parth was worried in connection with his future. Princess Nirupma told him to stay there and she would make him Commander-in-chief. He laughed loudly and clasped her in his arms. She felt that there was a lot of strength in his iron-like body. It felt good to be embraced by him. Parth was given all amenities. There was a very big lake in the palace surrounded by a railing and a bridge over it and another parallel lake that was connected to the lake from where the water came. There were thick pipes lying between the two pools. There was also a swimming pool and about 50 people were employed to look after the arrangement here.

That day both of them roamed around a lot and became dead tired. They did some horse riding too when they returned to the palace, while returning the jeep was being driven at a high speed . PArth was in the driving seat and the princess was sitting beside him wearing a coca-cola colored sari. Her hair was falling to her shoulders and she was talking to him with small hand gestures. She was telling him about the wild animals and the Naxalite attacks. Suddenly a soldier in military uniform gestured to them with his hand. Parth started reducing the speed of the jeep, but the soldier wanted them to continue ahead. But Parth did not understand and brought the jeep to a halt near where he was standing.

"Hello, what is the matter?"

"Sir, my daughter is not well, please take her to the hospital. My name is Bheem Singh."

The princess said, " But you had been relieved of your job."

"Yes Madam, but please help me at this time and make some arrangement."

"Have pity on me."

"Parth, please start the car, Parth was hearing the conversation."

The man looked at Parth in desperation and Parth asked him where his daughter was and the man replied that she was lying outside the house. Parth asked the princess to sit in the girl on the back seat of the car but she was unwilling so he forcibly made her sit there and made his way to the house. The girl was put in the jeep. The princess did not like all this but she was helpless to say anything. She was aware of PArth's nature.

The hospital was a mile away, as soon as the jeep entered the hospital compound there was activity everywhere. The girl was immediately attended to. The hospital in-charge came and insisted that they take rest.

PArth gave his assent by nodding his head and helped Nirupama to get down from the car. They reached the guestroom that was very well decorated. Tea and snacks were served. The female doctor served them tea, PArth asked after the welfare of the girl.

The girl is very weak, she was suffering from jaundice, but she is ok now.

Parth said he wanted to meet the girl and went to the ward where the girl was lying on a bed. She was constantly closing and opening her eyes.

PArth put a hand on her forehead and said that she would be ok, and then they would all play and enjoy themselves. BhimSingh told Parth that if he was in need of anything he should let him know. The princess was feeling uneasy because people of the palace and commoners do not meet each other socially and she felt that her father might get angry, but she was unable to explain to Parth.

Bhim Singh expressed his thanks by folding his hands. Parth tried to give him 500 rupees which he refused to accept. Then PArth asked him how he was managing without getting a salary, his eyes welled up but he did not say anything. PArth told him to come and meet him the next morning. He told PArth that he had had been thrown out from the job and denied entry into the palace.

PArth became quiet and the scene of his court martial appeared before his eyes.

The princess did not like all this but as has been said before she was totally helpless because she did not want to let Parth feel insulted.

"Sir, how can I come?"

"I will come to your house then."

The princess said, "Ok, you can come to the palace, but I will have to ask my father first."

PArth said, "no, I will come to your house tomorrow. Nirupama, I don't want to be an obstacle in any of your business, I will meet him here in the hospital itself."

BhimSingh fell at Parth's feet and said, " You are like God to me, I will come and stand outside the palace."

"Ok, I will meet you at eleven sharp because I have to go to Delhi by the night flight."

"Nirupama, "You will go tomorrow."

"Yes, tomorrow itself."

"I was hoping that you would stay for a few days and we could go for outings."

"No, I have but one objective."

"What is that?"

"You will come to know when the time comes."

"You became so emotional for an ordinary soldier."

"I saw truth and loyalty in his eyes and helplessness; I have also faced such situations."

"I could have asked my father to reinstate him to his job. Why take all this bother?"

"There is no question of any botheration, it is of a soldier's mental trauma. As far as his job is concerned I too can give him a salary."

"Ok, have your way." She became normal and asked him if he had come with any particular motive.

"No,no. I came just to meet you. I like you a lot."

"Them marry me."

"Your father will not like me. You don't have the courage to oppose him. I don't have any fixed abode or work, anything can happen to me."

"Ok, leave it, let's go." They left for the palace.

The next day Captain Parth sent for Bhim Singh with the order that he should come to the Radha Krishna temple. They met in the garden adjoining the temple. Bhim Singh told him that Naxalite attacks happened quite frequently and they had a modern army and modern arms also.

"Why were you thrown out form your job?"

"Sir, I have always been the most loyal person for the raja sahib. I used to give him all the information. I came to know that Raja Saheb's brother-in-law was connected to some terror organization that wanted to kill him and get hold of all his property. He used to sell the costly guns, telescopic guns from the armoury to the terror organizations and also supplied them with explosives and this was gradually weakening the force of the Raja Saheb.

Mehar Singh started suspecting me and he secretly stashed away some weapons from the armoury in my house and complained to the Raja Saheb. Raja Saheb gave orders for a search and Mehar Singh's soldiers arrested me from my house.

An investigation took place and I could not prove myself innocent. A conspiracy was hatched and I was thrown out of my job. The palace can be attacked any time.

Captain PArth has his own unique method of doing things. He assured Bhim that he would restore his status to him and he should just obey his orders.

It was 11 at night and there was silence all around. Everyone was deep in sleep. The princess's room was next to her parents'. Suddenly it struck Captain Parth that this was an appropriate time to investigate the armoury of the Raja Saheb. He gave an envelope to a servant and told him to take it to the princess. At first he was reluctant to do so, but ultimately agreed to the task. The letter was in code language since he was fearful that if anyone read it the consequences would be disastrous.

The princess was deep in sleep. She was aroused by the knocking at her door, but she forced herself to get up and opened the door to find the servant with the letter in his hand. On reading the letter, the sleep vanished from her eyes. She quickly threw some water on her eyes and went to wake up her father. He was also astounded and immediately called Captain PArth to his room.

The captain said, " this is not the time to sleep, you should immediately go to the armory and take your brother-in-law into your custody. He has made deceitful plans in cahoots with Mehar Singh and has sent his family to a safe place. The king, queen and princess were lost in thought. They had no other alternative but to trust the Captain. The armoury should be inspected with great secrecy. They were astounded to find that the expensive telescopic revolvers, pistols and explosives were almost half in number. It was clear that the armoury in-charge was involved.. They could hardly believe their eyes.

 SACRIFICED LIFE

The suspected soldiers were rounded up and were brainwashed by Captain PArth who tried to reignite them with the feeling of nationalism. When the terrorist organizations got wind of this, they were enraged. They were wiped out under the able leadership of Captain PArth.

Captain PArth had been successful in his mission. The border had become secure and he quietly left the place.

Notorious area

In every country and area there are some places where there is a 'one man show' meaning that only one person's orders reign supreme. The public has to go with his wishes and any breach of orders means death.

Here it is very important to understand one thing and that is that some governments use ruthless terrorist organization for their own motives and then establish their own governments that are no less than dictatorships.

Terrorism takes birth from the womb of cruel governments. Terrorism further gains ground and becomes a monster for the entire human race. With the changing times, there has been a change in warfare also. Every religion and caste has its own opinion on war and peace and they all have different interpretations. The results of war are also a matter of serious thought.

When Parth was living in the ashram he was made aware of the power of the mind. He was also taught hypnotism. This gives the meditator a power that makes the onlookers see what he wants them to see. This is the use of a type of imaginary power in which eyes have an importance.

The meditator can use his powers in adverse circumstances too. The use of these powers for personal gain is not allowed and if he uses the powers he has to suffer the results.

Shrimadbhagwad Geeta First chapter first shloka. A broad explanation of the principle of duty. The sanctity or pollution of thoughts. It is believed that when bad qualities reach their limit, then the Supreme God has to come down to this earth in some form or the other and heed the prayers of the people.

When Captain PArth was a student, his colleague was a big gambler. He had a way with cards. He used to play in the hotels and always won. He used to get 255 shares of the winnings. Captain PArth learnt this art form him.

There was one city that touched the heights of culture and on the other hand one that scoffed at human culture where there were no rules and no law. It was a hub of liquor, gambling and prostitution and where it was difficult for a normal person to live. Most people were corruptPolice officers used to be insulted. It was the rule of criminals and normal life was insecure. A matter of tension for the Central government. It was done under the leadership of Mr. Ho. The entire city was under his control but he had some hotels too. The hotel's name was ho where all the wrong sins were committed. The hotel had all the amenities. Human trafficking also took place here. Ho had connections in Saudi Arabia. The sheikhs there were supplied with girls for which different methods were used. If reporters opened their mouths they were killed. The government was also helpless because many of the ministers were supporters of Ho.

The reporter Vishnu Prabhakar prepared the entire story of Mr. Ho. and gave it to the newspaper 'Amna Samna'. The editor did not publish the story and Vishnu Prabhakar was thrown out from his job. He was in dire straits. Complaining against Ho was like a death punishment.

Vishnu Prabhakar quietly left Delhi with his family. By coincidence the Captain was also travelling in the same bogey. When the train stopped at the outer at 2 o'clock, it was dark and the visibility was very low. IT did not take long for Parth to realize that the goons of Ho had come to kill Vishnu Prabhakar. There were about 7 to 8 people. They were checking the travellers. PArth made Vishnu Prabhakar lied down on his seat and himself went and sat on his seat.

Last journey

Even after the court martial of Captain PArth, the Indian government was compelled to take his services secretly. There were many reasons for this. One was that RAW and many other secret agencies of India were giving out secret news about India-Captain Parth has saved India from many dangers and had given punishment to tyrants himself that was totally unconstitutional.

Many countries were against the working style of Captain Parth. India's secret pact with other countries was also being affected. There were two groups in the defense department-one was in favor of Parth and the other was against him.

The philosophical explanation for Captain Parth's ideology- The question is whether a soldier should have the right to make his own decisions or to follow the orders or to follow orders blindly.

 SACRIFICED LIFE

How to win a war when you are not so capable? Should Guerilla warfare be used or dirty politics or some other alternative? One's country should face minimum losses and the enemy country should suffer maximum losses. Can the third world war be stopped? There can be reasons for war. The expansionist policy of communism. The tendency of countries to prove themselves as the best and the continuation of cold war for a long time. To overlook or ignore the …principle.

Some of the reasons for war are religious discords, show of arrogance and the clash of different cultures. One needs to find out why nations tend to become obstinate about their opinions.

America saw that some terrorist organizations were backing Captain PArth that had broken ties with America. There was pressure to announce Captain PArth as a terrorist. The Indian government was in a dilemma.

Who is a betrayer and who is a Nationalist? Who is religious and who is an atheist? Who is a humanist and who is a terrorist? Who is an extremist? All these definitions have been formed according to some standards. It is difficult to categorize people in haste.

Sometimes nationalists are proved to be traitors and vice versa. This is not only in India but in other countries also.

Nobody had an answer to Captain PArth's opposing voice. Nobody ever asked whether Subhash Chandra Bose was a traitor. Were Chandra Shekhar Azad, Bhagat Singh and Rajguru traitors? There were many such names who sacrificed themselves to the freedom struggle.

There are such people in all countries who have gladly shed every drop of blood to protect their country. There have been poets and philosophers who were given death, were they traitors?

Jesus Christ, Socrates, Meera and Mosile (Africa) were given death but they are alive today. There are some names that have done a lot for the world like Martin Luther, Abraham Lincoln, Mahatma Gandhi, Dayanand Saraswati, Dr. Shyama Prasad Mukherjee, Smt. Indira Gandhi, Rajiv Gandhi, etc, but they died in unnatural circumstances and we should deliberate upon it.

Vanshika was an IPS officer and the daughter of Varsha and Vansh. She was working on a special mission. She could not establish contact with Captain Parth, and neither could he.

Both had telepathic conversations with each other at about 2 or 3 o'clock at night. A saint by the name of Ramanand was living in a temple with a fake ID. He used to keep an eye on world happenings from there. He gave the news to Vanshika that the President should be saved. Since his security guard was a terrorist group. The incident was going to take place at 11.30 that night. The entire information was in code.

She could not have worked alone and wanted to meet the Home Minister but he had gone abroad. IT also came to be known that a Union Minister was involved with a terrorist group. The Honorable Prime Minister was on a tour of Uttar Pradesh, she immediately got into touch with his security guard and Vanshika met him in the form of a reporter. She gave the interview questionnaire and feel down unconscious, there was chaos. The Prime Minister understood the gravity of the situation and transferred the information to the secret department.

The President was saved. The contribution of PArth and Vanshika in the national interest cannot be forgotten.

When the Prime Minister went to meet Vanshika, a lot of officials were already there. She started sobbing-she wanted to say Captain Parth, but the Prime Minister kept his hand on her mouth and patted her head saying that everything was alright.

The Prime Minister was interviewed. Dhruva- Many secrets have to be kept as secrets for the good of the country. Ram never claimed to be God. Why? He was a king. It is easy to be a king but very difficult to shoulder the responsibilities.

All the secret agencies and terrorist organizations of the world had started falling apart. Where is Captain PArth? Had the earth swallowed him or the sky?

If you ever find out, please do meet.

Captain PArth died for the country and live for the country.

Jai Hind, Jai Bharat,

I salute Captain Parth.

* * *